# MARKET PLACE 3.0

# MARKET PLACE 3.0

## REWRITING THE RULES OF BORDERLESS BUSINESS

## HIROSHI MIKITANI

palgrave
macmillan

MARKETPLACE 3.0
Copyright © Hiroshi Mikitani, 2013.

First published in hardcover in 2013 by PALGRAVE MACMILLAN® in
the United States—a division of St. Martin's Press LLC, 175 Fifth Avenue,
New York, NY 10010.

Where this book is distributed in the UK, Europe and the rest of the
world, this is by Palgrave Macmillan, a division of Macmillan Publishers
Limited, registered in England, company number 785998, of Houndmills,
Basingstoke, Hampshire RG21 6XS.

Palgrave Macmillan is the global academic imprint of the above
companies and has companies and representatives throughout the world.

Palgrave® and Macmillan® are registered trademarks in the United
States, the United Kingdom, Europe and other countries.

ISBN: 978-1-137-27918-7

Library of Congress Cataloging-in-Publication Data

Mikitani, Hiroshi.
Marketplace 3.0 : rewriting the rules of borderless business / Hiroshi
Mikitani.
     p.   cm.
1. Electronic commerce—Management. 2. Business enterprises—
Computer networks—Management. 3. Business logistics—Management.
4. International business enterprises—Management. I. Title.
HF5548.32.M537   2013
658.8'72—dc23
                                                              2012035393

A catalogue record of the book is available from the British Library.

Design by Letra Libre, Inc.

First PALGRAVE MACMILLAN paperback edition: July 2014

10  9  8  7  6  5  4  3  2  1

Printed in the United States of America.

# CONTENTS

# INTRODUCTION

# WHY REWRITE THE RULES?

In 1996, at the age of thirty-one, I did the unthinkable. I quit my job at the Industrial Bank of Japan.

To say this broke a "rule" of traditional Japanese corporate behavior would be an understatement. The ladder of success in Japan is firmly established and has been long revered: succeed in school, secure a position at a prestigious company, work your way up, and tie your success to the company's. This is the very definition of achievement in Japanese business. It is what countless students look toward when they bury themselves in their books every day.

And yet, when I resigned, few who knew me were surprised.

"We thought you might do this," my father told me.

"You will be back to do business with us one day," my superiors at IBJ said.

"It's just Mikitani—what do you expect?" said many of my friends and colleagues.

My decision had not been hasty. It was one I had been pondering that year in the wake of a dramatic event in my life. In 1995, the Hanshin Earthquake struck western Japan, devastating the city where I had grown up—where my parents and other relatives still resided. While my parents survived, some of my other relatives did not. I remember desperately searching for my aunt and uncle after the quake, finally finding their bodies at a local school that had been converted to a temporary morgue. I realized in those days how tenuous life is, how we have only one life and it must be lived to the fullest—not someday, but now.

My experience after the earthquake helped to cement what had long been my process. Over the course of my life, from my student days through the early years of starting my company to my status today as a CEO and corporate leader, I have viewed most rules as there to be challenged and, when necessary, rewritten. From the pieces, we can fashion new and better ways to achieve success.

I started down this path early. In high school, I joined the tennis team. I didn't last very long—no fault of my playing skills, but rather because I was unwilling to follow the tradition at the club that required younger players to serve as ball boys for senior players. Later, at university, when I rose to the rank of team captain, the first thing I did was abolish the rule. Everyone could chase his or her own tennis balls with equal results. The rule had no point; it needed to go.

In the early days of Rakuten, when we launched our first Internet mall, we gave our retailers the ability to customize their sites. They could edit, market, price, and function according to their own goals and processes. It was outrageous, even to the retailers we recruited to be our first merchants. They'd never heard of such a thing. Malls, retail industry veterans said, needed to be standardized and controlled. But this rule of standardization felt antiquated to me. It was time for it to be rewritten.

Here's a more recent one: in Japanese companies, conduct dictates that everyone do business in Japanese. I broke that rule when I announced last year that the first and only language of Rakuten would be English. I am still in the process of dismantling the old system in favor of my new vision, and not everyone is happy about it. Rule breaking isn't always quick and easy.

Still, it is necessary in the changing world we inhabit today. At Rakuten, we think of the company as being on the cutting edge of coming change. If 2.0 described the way digital life shifted to the web, then 3.0 is the next sea change—the evolution driven by personalization, intelligent search, and user behavior. We give this book the tag of 3.0 to establish its place in the digital continuum and position it to drive the online experience forward. There is more change ahead.

I'm sure I will face and challenge many more rules on the road ahead. What began as my personal philosophy of success has morphed into my corporate mission and worldview.

But to break rules well, it must be done right. In this book, I will lay out why I do it, how I do it, and how this strategy underlies all my personal and professional success. It is my hope that others will look at the path I am taking and see it as a possibility for their own work.

I am not suggesting a business world with no rules. Far from it. My own company is as structured and process oriented as any. I believe in guidelines for everything, from meeting planning to new product introduction. There is no profit in anarchy.

However, it has been my experience that blind adherence to conventional wisdom—the way things have always been done—is a shackle on business. Old rules may have gotten us to a certain level of success, but in order to move forward, some must be tossed aside. Often these rules are long-standing, revered, and deeply entwined with the culture of the company and even the country. They are not easily challenged. They are not easily changed. But if we can successfully reconfigure old ways of thinking and communicating, the results can be dramatic. That has been my experience. That has been the Rakuten experience. It is my hope to see that experience replicated many times, all over the world.

# ONE

# REWRITING THE RULES OF LANGUAGE

## OUR JOURNEY TO ENGLISHNIZATION

Think back to your student days, to your adolescence. Think back to what you studied during those years. Your schedule probably included math, science, literature, history. It's also likely you studied a foreign language.

In your language class, perhaps you learned basic conversation—phrases a tourist would use. Perhaps you even read some literature written in that language or studied the culture. At some point, you achieved proficiency in the subject, then left it behind.

Now, these many years later, imagine you came to work one morning and the boss announced that the entire corporation would be converting every aspect of the business to that language, dimly remembered from your teenage years. Right now. Today. Your native language was out; the foreign language had replaced it.

How would you feel after hearing that announcement?

Even if you were a straight-A student back in your school days, you'd probably be pretty shocked. I know. This is what I saw on all of my employees' faces the day I announced, in 2010, that Rakuten would embark on a journey I call Englishnization. I told my seven thousand employees—mostly native Japanese speakers—that we would stop what they had been doing all their working lives and immediately transition to doing business in English.

I made this announcement in English. I held that day's board meeting in English. Within twenty-four hours of my announcement, all the signs in the headquarters, from the elevators to the cafeteria, had been switched over from Japanese to English. Word rippled from Rakuten headquarters in Tokyo to the global offices in France, the United States, and Taiwan. I was 100 percent serious. Rakuten would have a new official language.

I knew my announcement would be met with skepticism and even bitterness. A fellow Japanese CEO even called my plan "stupid." Japanese executives do not generally criticize one another in the press, so the fact that they printed it was a huge indication of just how controversial my idea was.

I accepted the blowback, but I didn't let it change my mind. I knew Englishnization was not just a good idea but a critical move. I was not just making a change; I was making a save. This had to be done, and done quickly. The future of Rakuten and the future of Japanese business were at stake. I could even see that the progress of globalization—the way by which the world will do business as one—rested on this concept moving forward. I was not deterred. Englishnization is a radical idea. It is so unprecedented, I needed to invent a word to embody it. But it is far more than a communications strategy. I launched it to disrupt a doomed process and replace it with a faster, more global, and more borderless functionality. In this chapter, I will take you through my thinking, Rakuten's experience, and why even after all that has happened, I believe that Englishnization is not just smart, but necessary. And not just for Rakuten, but for society at large.

## WHY ENGLISH?

Why not Chinese? Many more people on the planet speak Chinese.

I didn't choose English based on the number of English speakers in the world—although it is significant. I chose English for several other reasons.

The first has to do with a business trend. English is the common language of global business. When speakers of all languages come together in commerce, English is most often the language they share. This is especially true in finance and engineering. Many top performers in these industries came up through English-language schools and universities. They likely came from many countries with many different language traditions, but the language of the lab, the conference room, and the trade show was English. They were doing business in English all over the world. Except in Japan.

As an island nation, Japan had managed to create its own linguistic bubble. While Japanese students were required to study about six years of English in middle and high school, they were never pressed to continue the study, and as a result, few adults could converse in English. Certainly, few Japanese were ever asked to conduct complex or demanding workplace tasks in English. Because Japan's own economy is substantial, most of its citizens can go through their business lives communicating only in Japanese. It has been that way for quite some time.

But globalization changed that matrix. The world was moving to a more borderless economic experience, and Japanese companies, clinging to Japanese language, were being left out. I could see that clearly from the executive perch. We were not communicating with the necessary speed and effectiveness, because we were insisting on a workplace of Japanese language. Just the act of translation added time to any process. It was time we no longer had. When I looked beyond the borders of my company and my country, it was clear we could not afford to sit out the global trend.

There is another reason, one more entwined in the intricacies of the two languages, that led me to English. Japanese is a language steeped in hierarchical structure. In Japanese conversation, there is often a power relationship unfolding. Speakers may need to clarify age, academic background, and bloodline—all through word choice, sentence structure, and the give-and-take of conversation. This is a part of the language that Japanese speakers are very aware of and engage in every day.

English, on the other hand, is a language with few power markers. By using English, I believed we could break down barriers and work more quickly. The move would be more than just linguistic; it would be cultural. Using English would allow us to take advantage of two key functions of English communication—speed and utility—and of a language that is not restrained by cultural norms.

## MY OWN HISTORY WITH ENGLISH

Englishnization was not born out of my personal affection for the language. I do not hold it above other languages as better or more beautiful. English, for me, has always been a language of utility.

My first direct exposure came at age seven, when I lived with my parents in Connecticut. My father was a visiting scholar at Yale University. I entered an English-speaking school environment with three English words: *yes*, *no*, and *bathroom*. We lived in the United States for two years, and as children do, I quickly picked up the conversation skills of my schoolmates.

When I returned to Japan with my family, my conversation skills faded and I became like most Japanese students: proficient in technical written English—in grammar and spelling and written conventions. But the speaking skills, not especially valued in my surroundings, I lost. It wasn't until university, when I set my sights on going to the United States to study business in graduate school, that I focused my efforts on improving all aspects of my English skills. I did it because I had a goal I wanted to achieve, and English was a necessary tool to achieve it. When I developed Englishnization for Rakuten, I went through the same process. But instead of setting a goal for myself, I set it for the entire company.

## MY AHA MOMENT

While the development of my English skills may have been gradual, my vision for Englishnization was not. It hit me with such clarity and intensity that I did not spend time researching and reviewing it. I simply moved forward.

I had been thinking about how we could become a more successful global company. I was thinking about the huge language barrier that had developed between our headquarters and our offices in subsidiaries outside Japan. The more we expanded in the world, the more often this language barrier became an issue. In 2005, Rakuten purchased the major U.S. affiliate-marketing company LinkShare Corporation. We moved into Taiwan in 2008 and Thailand in 2009, establishing Internet shopping malls in each market much like Rakuten Ichiba in Japan. Business was going well, but I couldn't help but think that we could be operating more efficiently than we were. It began to creep into my thinking that our inefficiencies were rooted in our use of language.

Take training, for example. Say that we want to have a staff member from one of our overseas subsidiaries or affiliate companies come to Japan to learn about the Rakuten Ichiba business model. In such cases, it used to be that we would have them speak with the people in charge of each department in Japan through an interpreter. The placement of an interpreter between the two parties slowed the pace of mutual understanding. There was no sense of speed, and beyond that, the interpretation made it difficult for the two sides to feel that they were working on the same team.

This worked against the core themes of our company. As we expand, the entire workflow of each member of Rakuten is completely integrated into our IT system. That might not surprise anyone, given that we are an Internet company. But what I mean is that, unlike in the past when we communicated with telephones and fax machines, these days all our communication is done via email or our in-house social network.

Yet as we were striving for full integration, we were hitting a language barrier. Even though I can communicate over the Internet with all the group companies—not just in Japan but subsidiaries abroad as well—in the past, employees overseas received my messages through interpretation or translations. In the reverse direction too, the messages from abroad would be translated from English into Japanese and passed on to the employees in Japan. This took time and effort. Despite having an infrastructure in place that should have allowed us to communicate with one another instantaneously, we weren't making effective use of it.

What's more, I could look ahead and see that this issue would grow only more problematic. I knew that if we were to continue to create original services, we would need to hire the best and the brightest from all over the world, not just those from Japan. The Japanese language made that difficult. I couldn't stand the idea that we would be forced to abandon hiring a promising candidate just because they couldn't speak any Japanese. And at the same time, I knew we needed to increase the number of employees in the company who could speak English. The more I thought about it, the more concerned I became. Up until that point, I had thought that we could continue to do business in Japanese and that, if anything, we didn't even really need English. I was so sure of this that I had even ordered foreign employees at Rakuten to take Japanese lessons. But as we shifted toward a stage in which we would need to get serious about overseas expansion, I realized that the ability to communicate in English was an absolute necessity if we were to operate globally.

The solution came to me as I watched individuals we had recruited from abroad make the transition to Rakuten. As we became more global, more people from other countries and other language traditions joined our firm, and I began to see that what we, in Japan, considered an insurmountable challenge was not viewed the same way in other cultures. I was impressed, for example, at the speed with which engineers we hired from India were learning Japanese. Within months of their hiring, they were conversant. I could see now that smart, motivated individuals could achieve proficiency in a new language in a relatively short period of time. So when the idea for Englishnization struck me, I seized on this evidence. As a lifelong entrepreneur, I am used to coming up with an idea one day and jumping off the cliff with it the next. I go straight from idea to action. I did not commission a study, organize a research group, or take a poll. If I had asked one hundred people about my idea to communicate in English, ninety-nine of them would have told me I was crazy. But they would have been wrong. And so I did not waste time in discussions that I knew would resist the scope and challenge of my plan. I knew it sounded crazy, but I also knew it was the right answer. Without any preparation, I told my executives that I wanted to do this at our next regular Monday meeting.

And then, perhaps even more ambitiously, I set a deadline. Two years from my announcement, all Rakuten employees would be required to score above 600 on the 990-point TOEIC (Test of English for International Communication) exam. Managers would have to achieve a much higher TOEIC score; junior managers would be required to have a score of 650, mid-level managers a score of 700, and upper-level managers a score of 750. Those who failed would risk being passed over for promotion or being demoted.

## THE PLAN

We implemented Englishnization in three phases.

Phase 1 consisted of assessment testing. This included the TOEIC—a two-hour test of English reading and listening comprehension. In many Japanese firms, the testing would likely take place only at the end of the process. But I wanted Englishnization to follow a scientific approach, whereby we first understood our baseline capabilities. Employees with low scores were required to take a computer-administered exam monthly, to inspire them and monitor their progress.

Phase 2 focused on English-language education. We brought in guest lecturers and held other events to engage the staff in the Englishnization process. We encouraged employees to enroll in English-language classes. We also made changes within our company. We changed the signage in the headquarters and the language of documents, both internal and external. I spoke in English to employees no matter where I was in the world—Japan, Indonesia, Brazil . . .

Phase 3 aimed to get people using their English skills in the workplace. Evaluators sat in on business meetings to give feedback on usage. Discussions were organized to encourage employees to engage in English with one another.

## WHAT HAPPENED NEXT?

The impact of Englishnization began immediately and has not let up. It became a force within the company and has had ripple effects outside our corporate boundaries, even around the world.

The first result came mere hours after my initial announcement. Rakuten had spent the past year making a series of acquisitions and other expansions. We had grown and evolved

and introduced a host of new products. But nothing cata-
pulted our brand as quickly and as surely into the spotlight as
Englishnization. Immediately we were an international story.

The global media community was fascinated. More than
one hundred stories appeared, in outlets ranging from CNN
to the *Wall Street Journal*, as well as leading Asian sources.
And as I mentioned, some of my colleagues in Japan were not
impressed, and their comments to journalists only fueled the
chatter. Englishnization drew more attention than any of our
recent overseas acquisitions, no matter how big. My head of
media and advertising cheered this jump start to our international brand. He said we hadn't gotten this much positive attention since I'd purchased a baseball team seven years earlier.

Being this kind of story has its pros and cons. It can be
a distraction—a focus on just one element of our company,
rather than on the organic whole. But it can also be a great
positive. With Englishnization, Rakuten's profile rose significantly on the global radar. If we were well-known before in
Japan and to our own international partners, we were now
far more visible around the world. Englishnization positioned
Rakuten as a company ready and able to do business with
the global community. We were not an island company in an
island nation. We were part of the global conversation. This
helped us negotiate deals, attract top talent to our company
from the global pool, and become a leading voice in international business.

Englishnization also made us a company to watch. When
companies do interesting and cutting-edge things, other firms

watch and learn from their experiences. When we launched
Englishnization, we became one of those firms. I knew this
for certain when my alma mater, Harvard Business School,
approached me about making Rakuten and Englishnization
the subject of one of its case studies.

Many companies dream of being the subject of an HBS
case study. It is a mark of distinction to be singled out as worthy of examination by the best minds in business. When HBS
came calling, it underscored that what we were attempting
at Rakuten was not just an internal corporate project, but a
seismic industry shift. We were not undertaking this experiment just for our own edification, or even our own bottom
line. Now we were also poised to be a teaching tool for the
world's business community.

## ENGLISHNIZATION'S IMPACT

Englishnization quickly reshaped our internal communication. I see the impact in daily interactions. I was at our subsid-
iary in Paris recently, and a question arose for our marketing
team. Before Englishnization, we would have had to search
for someone who spoke English to facilitate the process of
answering. Now the person with the question can pick up the
phone and ask anyone—without losing a moment. It is an
undeniable improvement.

Not all improvements are immediately cheered, however.
For example, our U.S. employees, based in New York, found
they had to extend their own work hours to accommodate

the uptick in calls coming in from Japan at late hours. Pre-Englishnization, there was less person-to-person contact. Communication was often executed via email and memo to allow time for translation. U.S. workers had less reason to be by the phone, since any communication with Japan might take a day or two to unfold. With Englishnization under way, the phones rang more often. Communication was more immediate. Perhaps that's not good if you're working on the East Coast and trying to get home early. But for the business, it was a plus. Interactions between employees in different counties that used to take two or three days could now take two or three minutes. The improvement in speed was dramatic, to say the least.

But it was not easy. In the first week after making the declaration on Englishnization, the materials and presentations at board meetings were switched into English. As they say in Japan, "Let he who is the first to suggest something, be the first to do it."

What troubled people the most at first was being asked questions. Things went smoothly when questions along the lines of those thought up beforehand were asked, but on occasion people were asked about completely unexpected matters. Answering a question off the cuff in English requires a certain level of expressiveness.

At first, it was very common for those executives who were poor at English to hesitate or stutter when answering. Meetings often felt awkward. There were even some executives who would ask if it was all right to say certain things in

Japanese and then immediately switch to English. Of course, my answer was always no. Naturally, there are certain phrases relating to matters such as Japanese legal documents or documents specific to domestic customers and services that are difficult to translate into English and for which there is no choice but to use Japanese. But aside from these terms, I asked that everything be communicated in English.

In return for not allowing Japanese, even if the speaker was at a complete loss for words, I waited patiently until they said something, and then tried to lend them a hand by suggesting what I thought they might be trying to say. There is nothing strange about people not being able to participate in meetings in English in the beginning. I felt that the important thing was to first have people get used to the idea itself.

The first board meeting we held that April took four hours to complete. This is double the time normally required. But the slowdown was temporary. And soon, within the company, personal success stories began to emerge. We had one manager who initially had little interest in improving his English. When I made my announcement, he assumed this would mean he'd leave the company when my deadline arrived. He believed the emphasis on English, particularly for employees who would not necessarily use it in their everyday jobs, was a distraction for the firm.

But his eyes were opened when he—at the urging of his supervisor—took time to attend an intensive English-language school in the Philippines. There he met students from other countries—Korea and China, for example—who were committed to learning English to advance their careers and the fortune of their companies in the global marketplace. This experience gave him the global perspective I had long been advocating: the vision of Japan engaging the world's businesses, and not remaining confined to our island and our domestic economy. This particular manger saw his TOEIC score jump 250 points in a matter of months. But more importantly, his outlook was transformed. English didn't just improve his standing in his company. It improved his company's standing in the world. This was a hugely motivational realization.

It is my broader goal to model this process for other companies in Japan. Like the manager who assumed Englishnization was a distraction, many firms in Japan are content to do business within our national borders, and they pay little heed to global trends. Englishnization does more than create a common language for employees. It opens their eyes to what is going on beyond the borders of the Japanese-speaking world in a new and dramatic way.

Just by implementing Englishnization in my own firm, I planted the idea that it could happen in other companies. And sure enough, I began to see Englishnization take on a bigger role—a leadership role—in the Japanese economy. I quickly became a spokesman for the concept. More and more, I was asked to participate in global discussions about the role of language and communication in business, and how Japanese companies must change to succeed in the new global economy. It has been an exciting development, and I have great hopes that it is not just a business discussion, but a harbinger of the New Japan—a fundamental shift in the way the country participates on the global stage.

## THE CHALLENGES

For all the positive impact of Englishnization, it has not been easy. When asked whether any aspect of the process has surprised me so far, I say that it created more stress than I anticipated—stress on individuals and also stress on the company.

The biggest challenge was time. I had set an aggressive schedule, but of course Rakuten employees still had their jobs to do. Employees were asked to study English on their own time—we set aside conference rooms for this purpose. We negotiated discounts with language classes for after-hours instruction. It was not a popular arrangement. I heard quite a bit about the stress that Englishnization was causing. Employees complained that they lost family time, that they lost sleep.

I sympathized. But I did not back off from my goal. It was not a small change in our business; it was a revolutionary one. Nothing revolutionary comes easily.

Another challenge was productivity. I couldn't deny that, as we pressed native Japanese speakers to do business in English, productivity temporarily suffered. Employees took longer to accomplish tasks.

Finally, I had to face the cultural impact of what I had ordered. By implementing Englishnization, I had disrupted a traditional hierarchy in my company and, indeed, in many companies. When I insisted we move to English, those with existing English skills gained status at the expense of those who were less skilled. Imagine, for instance, a work group led by a senior manager in his forties and filled out by younger employees; this could be a significant shift. The younger employees, closer to their school days, may well have better English skills than their manager. The manager, once comfortably in control of his team, may now find that because his English is not as strong, he feels less confident in his leadership role and perhaps even threatened by his more proficient subordinates. The balance of power also shifted on a global scale. Native English speakers, or individuals from a country with a stronger tradition in English-language study, found they had an edge in Rakuten that they didn't have before. Whether or not this was technically true, it was certainly a concern that flowed through the employee population. It was an issue that worried them and created concerns that had not been present before.

Ultimately, I had to find a way to encourage my employees to practice their English where everyone in the workplace could see them. In Japanese society, it is very important to avoid a loss of "face," or reputation. It became clear that some Rakuten employees were avoiding practicing their English in the workplace because it was not perfect, and they feared embarrassment by their grammatical errors. I tried to provide leadership in this area. I joked that the corporate standard at Rakuten was not English but poor English. I began to understand that my role had to be more than simply conceiving and launching Englishnization. I would have to participate as well—coax it along.

In the year after the announcement, even as everyone wrestled with the enormity of the task, I could already see positive results. But I also learned how much more it would take for the project to succeed on the global scale I envisioned.

Perhaps this is where I had my greatest moments of learning. Toward the end of the first year of the project, I began to realize the enormity of the task. People needed more time to study and reach their required targets. The Great East Japan Earthquake and the impact of the tsunami prompted me to push back the deadline of the project by three months. It was still imperative that we be fully fluent as soon as possible. But every grand experiment at some point requires patience, flexibility, and realism.

I hold fast to my Englishnization goals because it is a necessary change, for all of us. I refuse to give up on anybody. I'm determined to do everything I can to help everyone meet the goal. I committed to additional resources for Englishnization, such as free lessons to those who needed them. We can't let anyone drop out if we can prevent it, because there is more at stake here than just the success of Rakuten.

I am proud of our results thus far. More than 90 percent of our staff has achieved the test scores we set. This is good news, but also a reminder that we must continue our efforts both for the sake of Rakuten and for the example we set for other companies. This is critical for Japan. We are thirteenth among Asian countries when it comes to English-language learning. We are behind China. We are behind Korea. We are way behind countries such as Singapore, Taiwan, and Indonesia. One of my greatest fears is that this is by design—a strategy to keep Japan the way it is now, in a bubble, not fully participating in the global community. By emphasizing the Japanese language, Japanese media and Japanese bureaucrats exert enormous control over Japanese citizens. Individual Japanese are not fully aware of what is going on beyond our borders. Some may see this as a way to protect the Japan of today, but I believe it is one of the reasons why some conservative people do not want to enhance English education.

But that plan is already doomed. The globalization of business, of communication, of all types of marketplace interaction today, makes this kind of isolation—this frozen-in-time quality—impossible.

The Internet has changed the world's economy profoundly and permanently. Economies that once functioned within national boarders are now intertwined, thanks to e-commerce and the free flow of information. That means any company, anywhere, is a global company, whether or not that was in the original business plan. None of us can escape the world around us.

National borders that once created protected economies are fading. Rakuten must adapt to this. Japan must adapt to this. All the world's businesses must adapt to this. The change has already happened. What remains to be seen is how we will respond.

This is why I cannot give up. Not on the Englishnization process, and not on any of my employees who are trying so hard to learn and achieve. My critics may think I'm selfish, and they may say I'm crazy. But deep down, they all know it is a necessary struggle. They are all watching to see how we do it. It is my goal to make Rakuten the example for others to follow, and I have no doubt they will. They have to. The global marketplace demands the speed of a single language. There is no time for translation, no time for misunderstanding. There can be only clarity and speed. The global economy depends on it.

## TRY THE RAKUTEN WAY

- Imagine your global business unified by language. Imagine if you did not have to rely upon the happy accident of easy communication, but sought to institutionalize a common language. How much time would be saved? What innovations would be possible?

- Consider how you might persuade your team or your company to undertake a task as big and as potentially game-changing as Englishnization. How would you motivate them? How would you lead this transformation?

- What would be the role of your company on the global stage if you achieved Englishnization? What position would your firm hold in the global business landscape?

# TWO

# REWRITING THE RULES OF POWER

## THE WISDOM OF EMPOWERMENT

There was once a small rice merchant in the south of Japan. His family had been in the business of growing and selling rice for three generations, a proud and distinguished tradition. But tough economic times were challenging him, and he was unable to expand his business. It was shrinking. His own son, as a result, left home upon finishing his schooling, in order to find more profitable work in an office. This saddened the merchant—not only was he unable to create new prosperity for his business, but he was unable to keep his family together.

The merchant was visited one day by a salesman from Rakuten. The salesman arrived in his shop excited and perspiring, as though he had just climbed a mountain. And his manner was just as eager:

"I've come to show you the opportunity you've been hoping for. I'm here to invite you to join the Rakuten marketplace. I promise to do everything I can to help you expand your business. I will offer you my best advice, help you find new customers, and be your partner in this process. Let's run together!"

The rice merchant was suspicious—he had little experience with computers. But the salesman made good on his offer of help right from the start. He helped train the rice merchant on how to operate the computer, create a virtual presence for his business, and take advantage of the marketing and sales tools of the Rakuten mall. Soon the rice merchant was up and running in the virtual marketplace.

The rice merchant was passionate about his business. He did more than just throw up a web page. He added content. He typed in the story of his family business, the traditions that he had incorporated over the years, the reasons his rice was special. And he shared his hopes and dreams for his business and his family.

The virtual marketplace responded. The rice merchant began to field orders from faraway communities—cities to which he had never traveled, even customers outside Japan. His business, once stalled, began to grow again, and then to thrive. Soon, he had to bring in more help. His son returned from the city to rejoin the team. The rice merchant had succeeded in jump-starting his business, reuniting his family, and positioning his company for ongoing success.

This is one of my favorite stories from the early days of Rakuten. I tell it often to employees and in the speeches I give to business audiences. I love this story because it embodies one of the critical elements of my business process: empowerment.

Empowerment is a word that gets a lot of buzz in business circles today. But the kind of empowerment I'm talking about does not revolve around letting employees wear jeans or bring their dogs to the office or work from the corner coffee shop. Empowerment, as I see it, is not a nice add-on that allows employees to feel good on a daily basis. Instead, it is a core business strategy—one that pervades everything we do, from my office down through the ranks of all my employees and out into the merchant and vendor community. At Rakuten, empowerment is not a line in the human resources manual. It is our goal in everything we do and what sets us apart from many of our e-commerce competitors.

When you look at the story of the rice merchant, you can see the many functions of empowerment in our business. Rakuten empowered the salesman to make the trek from Tokyo to meet with a single merchant. The company empowered that salesman to promise to be that merchant's helper—including even the most basic computer support. Rakuten then empowered the rice merchant to express the true nature of his business via the Rakuten mall—no cookie-cutter templates for our merchants. Finally, and most significantly for me, Rakuten empowered the rice merchant to achieve his fondest dream: to find new growth for his business and make it so that his son would want to come home and pick up the family tradition. Rakuten didn't do that for him; we made it possible for him to do it for himself. When he looks back on this turn of events, he can take pride in his accomplishment. As his partner, we can too.

In this chapter, I will explore the concept of empowerment and how it runs through the veins of the Rakuten organization. It is my goal to demonstrate how empowerment fuels many functions of this company, and why it is a key strategy not just for us but for the future of global e-commerce. In these pages, we'll look at:

- How Rakuten empowers its customers (such as the rice merchant)
- How Rakuten empowers its employees (such as our salesmen)
- How Rakuten avoids chaos from empowerment by setting quantitative goals and using key performance indicators (KPIs)
- How empowerment can be a strategy for personal success (I'll use myself as a prime example)
- Why companies and individuals that embrace empowerment will be in a position to change the world

## EMPOWERING CUSTOMERS

While it may seem surprising now, the e-commerce industry did not embrace empowerment in the early days.

Certainly the growth of the Internet and the advent of the World Wide Web made it possible for individuals to set up shop online. There were many early pioneers who did just that. But the difficulty of being a sole proprietor in the virtual world quickly became clear: you may have the best product in the world, but if customers don't know you exist, you make no sales. This concern led quickly to online shopping malls.

Many of the biggest names in technology and media added online shopping mall developer to their list of activities. They created malls on the web and signed up merchants to fill their virtual storefronts. And one by one, they failed.

Let's look at one example. In 1996, IBM announced it would open World Avenue—a virtual shopping mall designed to give the sixteen initial retail clients access to the global marketplace via the World Wide Web. Some big names in retail signed up: L.L. Bean, Hudson's Bay, Gottschalks. It looked like the start of something big.

But less than a year after the debut, the project was discontinued. Why? The official reason was not enough customer traffic. But below the surface was a current of retailer dissatisfaction. The retail clients had been unhappy with IBM as a mall landlord. They did not appreciate the overlay of the IBM brand on their virtual stores. They chafed at IBM's presence as an intermediary in their sacrosanct relationship with customers. In short, they believed IBM was hurting more than it was helping. Why should they pay for some outside company to create a barrier between them and their customers? The retail tenants quickly abandoned World Avenue.

What had IBM done wrong? Frankly, the same thing many other technology and media companies did wrong when they first dabbled in e-commerce: they insisted on ruling with a heavy hand. They came into the project determined to demonstrate their dominance, and they exerted control every step of the way. The purpose of this, IBM and others insisted, was to maintain efficiency and cohesion. But merchants rebelled.

We got into e-commerce in 1997. (And when I say "we," I mean myself and my partner at the time.) We were no IBM or Microsoft, which had also tried and failed to launch an Internet mall. So I felt we needed a different strategy. I decided Rakuten's mall would offer the opposite of the big companies' malls. It would offer not a controlled storefront, but rather virtual empowerment.

From the start, Rakuten's mall was different. We offered our services for a monthly price of fifty thousand yen ($650) payable in two installments based on an annual subscription. This was a fraction of what the big Internet malls charged. We offered merchants the opportunity to customize their web presence, rather than to fit into one designed by us. In fact, we were so committed to this process of customization that we developed special tools to give these merchants (many of whom had limited computer skills) the chance to make their virtual storefronts look just as they wanted.

This was not easy. My other employee was better at programming than I was, so I presented him with a copy of *SQL for Dummies* to inspire him. But in the end, we had to go out and hire a tutor to teach us how to create the tools. This seemed like a lot of work at the time, but I knew it was critical. Empowerment starts with a mind-set of enabling the client. We didn't want just to collect the money to do this work for our merchants—we wanted them to be able to do it on their own.

We took the concept a step further with the communication between the merchant and the retail customer. In the original Internet mall construct—and indeed, still today in some of the other major e-commerce players—communication is controlled by the mall owner. The merchant does not have the ability to interact directly with the customer. Instead, all communication—orders, complaints, requests for information, etc.—is funneled through the mall operator.

This seemed to me like a tremendous waste of time and resources.

Why should I be answering the merchant's email? If a customer wants to know something specific about a product, he does not want to ask me. What do I know, sitting in my offices in Tokyo, about how the rice merchant in northern Japan ships his product? Or which among his products might be best for a particular customer? Or what makes his rice special? These are questions for the merchant, and the most efficient communication process possible is between the two parties themselves—without intermediaries.

We empower the merchant to manage his or her own communications, as well as empowering the customer to engage directly with the merchant.

This is not the way it's done throughout e-commerce, even today. Many small merchants have signed on with our competitors to gain access to the global Internet marketplace. But these major e-commerce players control much of the process, not the least of which is the communications avenue. All communications funnel through the e-commerce platform.

From web-page design to email to relationship management, we seek to be an empowering rather than a controlling force. The early Internet mall developers were certain that their merchants would not be able to handle life in the virtual marketplace. They were convinced that merchants needed structure, control, and limits. But they were wrong, as evidenced by the failure of so many Internet malls at the outset. Their need for control backfired. It wasn't profitable for the merchants, and it interfered with their long-term goals.

But when empowered by a virtual mall owner, retailers thrived. The rice merchant is a perfect example. Rakuten didn't just take him on as a client; we empowered him to be successful as a merchant, as a father, and as the custodian of his family's history and traditions. And he was far from our only example. More recently, Rakuten worked with a seller of pet clothing—everything from warm winter jackets to wedding dresses for canines attending their owners' nuptials. Perhaps one of the most significant ways Rakuten supported this business (called iDog) was to empower the owner to connect with her customers. The ways in which iDog (and iCat) customers communicate and engage with the stores are many. The owner and staff write frequently about their own pets and post the content to the website and e-newsletter. The site is full of photographs from happy customers of pets dressed up in iDog and iCat attire. The company even has a special program to use customer pets as official models. There are currently sixty regular models in use and a backlog of a thousand more who would love to see their pets on the site.

iDog succeeded in no small part because Rakuten did not interfere with the bonding between pet owners and retailer. We made it possible for those two entities to connect. Then we got out of the way and let the magic happen.

## EMPOWERING EMPLOYEES

As I said earlier, my definition of empowerment, when it comes to employees, may differ slightly from others'. "Empowerment" was a term that got a lot of lip service back during the dot-com era. Employers, eager to attract scarce technology talent, used empowerment as a lure. They promised quite a bit of personal freedom, from relaxed dress codes to remote work arrangements to flexible scheduling. This all fell under the banner of "employee empowerment." But is that really what the word means?

To my thinking, empowering employees is not about allowing them to make work more like home through decorations or pets or laptops. Instead, I see employee empowerment as a way to give workers the chance to do their best work—without limitations imposed by me or by other managers.

How does that happen?

The first way I approach this is through collaboration and team projects. At Rakuten, we encourage employees to work collaboratively to solve problems and find new opportunities. This becomes more of a challenge for me as a manager as the company grows. When I had one, two, ten employees, it was not hard to allow them to try new things. It was easy for me to keep track of what they were doing. Today, Rakuten has more than ten thousand employees in multiple countries. It's not possible to keep track of every movement. You might think that this requires more control and supervision to ensure that everyone is on track. But I go back to my philosophical passion for empowerment. I believe giving freedom is more important than maintaining control.

The second way to empower employees is by adopting a framework that never allows for ultimate failure and always allows for another try. When I explain this concept, I often talk about it in sports terms. Many people like to compare business and sports, and indeed there are many common concepts. But in sports, there are rules and limits, and I reject these confines in order to empower my employees. In baseball, for example, it's three strikes and you're out. At Rakuten, on the other hand, you can swing as many times as it takes. There is never any reason to leave the field in failure. If you miss, swing again.

One thing I made sure to do when I set up my business model was to create a structure in which we can always take another swing. This is a critical construct at Rakuten because it empowers my employees to never give up. If we are still in business, you are still empowered to go out there and take another swing at the ball. As long as you can try again, failure is impossible. But it's the responsibility of the senior manager to communicate that to employees.

A third step in employee empowerment is tied to my process of Englishnization. There are many good reasons to make English the language of the workplace, and one of them is its inherent directness. One of my senior executives especially values the use of English in the workplace because it is often the one thing that gets these young, eager recruits to step up and say confidently what they truly think and mean, rather than take a safe, neutral stance. He tells the following story:

> When I ask a new employee whether it will rain tomorrow, if he responds in Japanese he might say: "If it will be sunny, that will be good." He makes no commitment to telling me what I want to know. He has answered me and not answered me at the same time. The linguistic trends of spoken Japanese allow him to dodge and remain neutral.
>
> But I have asked for information, so this is not useful for me or for the company.
>
> Now, if I try the same question in English, I get a different response.
>
> "Will it rain tomorrow?"
>
> Following the conventions of English-language communication, the employee must now answer "Yes," "No," or "Maybe."
>
> Perhaps I will not get an accurate weather forecast, but the use of English in the workplace compels us all to be more direct in our communication, more concrete, less likely to avoid the confrontation of saying yes or no.

It is not easy to shake off the language traditions you have been raised with. By changing the language, I offer a chance to embrace new rules of communication. I empower us all to speak in the more direct, concrete tradition of English.

Employee empowerment also benefits the bottom line. It's my opinion that by allowing for collaboration and other empowered actions, we keep our best workers. If you use money as the only carrot to keep your best employees, eventually that employee will find more money elsewhere. It can't be your only retention strategy. If, on the other hand, you offer your best employee the chance to do his or her best work—in a collaborative work environment, with the understanding that he or she is empowered to try, explore, and create—then you have provided a real reason for that employee to stay.

## AVOIDING CHAOS

Many times when I talk about empowerment, I hear back from fellow businesspeople: That may work in your company. But in my firm, it would produce chaos. And it's true that simply allowing everyone to do anything they want would be chaotic. That's not what I advocate, or what we practice. Instead, we've found a way to empower employees while avoiding chaos. We simply merge our passion for empowerment with another company passion: measurement.

Metrics and measuring play a daily role in the way we approach motivation at Rakuten. We use them in a variety of ways to influence individuals, work groups, and the entire company to achieve their highest success.

Every business has its favorite acronyms. One you will hear often at Rakuten is KPI. It stands for "key performance indicator," a system we use to help employees set and achieve mid-term goals. I began to see the need for KPIs as Rakuten grew. As our goals became more complex, employees needed help staying motivated and focused. Big goals are important for an ambitious organization. But in order to accomplish these goals, you must outline the concrete steps toward achieving them in an understandable way. If your employees can't see the markers that tell them where they are going or how far they've come, the only result will be confusion. KPIs are your markers.

For example, you might use KPIs to measure how many deals a salesperson has made or how many new clients that person has signed. KPIs allow individual members of your organization to measure themselves and see the steps they must take to move the company toward its larger goals.

KPIs become increasingly important as a company grows. For employees, as the organization becomes bigger and bigger, the goals become bigger and smaller tasks can come to seem less important. An individual may start to feel that what he or she does is of less consequence to this larger whole. This feeling, if left unchecked, can spread among employees and threaten the forward progress of the entire organization. Certainly we have seen examples of big companies that seemed so powerful and yet lost their momentum. One reason is this sense of smallness that an individual employee may come to feel as the company looms large.

KPIs, therefore, can bridge the work of an individual to the larger work of the organization. It is the connection point between the small jobs an employee may do every day and the big goals the company may have in the coming years. Some KPIs are set by managers, but it's a tactic that employees can also use themselves to achieve personal goals. For example, our company began using an internal social networking site to help us share ideas and communicate across our growing organization. I have asked employees to post to this site often. But I have also seen individual employees set their own KPIs in order to remind them to do this. If they set a KPI to post a certain number of times a week, that moves them toward the smaller goal of individual participation, which helps Rakuten achieve its larger goal of maintaining a thriving internal social network.

But in addition to acting as a motivational tool, our devotion to metrics supports our larger efforts of empowerment. When you are open with numbers and let everyone know how well they are doing, how close or far they are to their goals, and what results their efforts are producing, you free them from the need to stand around and wait for orders or instructions. The numbers are there—they can be seen and understood by all. If your department is falling short on sales goals, you can see that in the numbers and you do not need to wait for instructions on what to do next.

Even as you set the day-to-day goals and the goals of the next few years, it is also important to set and measure your progress toward the big goals. And these goals should be specific and extraordinary. Consider when NASA said it would go to the moon. This seemed outlandish at the time. John F. Kennedy first announced on May 25, 1961, that by the end of the 1960s the United States would send a man to the moon. This came against the backdrop of a cultural phenomenon some called "Sputnik Shock," when the former Soviet Union succeeded in sending into space the first satellite, Sputnik. At that time, the United States had not yet been able to launch a satellite. The thought that their rival, the Soviet Union, had beaten them in sending a satellite into space shattered the public's confidence. It didn't help that a month before Kennedy's speech the Soviet Union had succeeded in sending up a manned satellite and making Yuri Gagarin the first man to ever look down upon the earth with his own eyes.

Kennedy's announcement to send a man to the moon was thus part of a plan to wipe away the shock that had spread across the United States. There has not been a speech since that so excited the American heart. Setting a timeframe of nine years, telling the public that the plan was to be accomplished not "someday" but "before this decade is out," was absolutely brilliant.

Perhaps it would have seemed more reasonable to say: "We will do our best work to explore space." Instead, NASA set the big, specific goal of the moon, and measured its own progress toward that goal. This is an important way to motivate employees. When you set small goals, you can feel the small positive rewards of achievement. When you set and move toward big goals, the rewards are much more intense. A coach who says, "Just try to run very fast" is not as influential as a coach who says, "Run to win!"

Even though these are long-term goals, they must also be measured and their progress tracked. Even if they seem far away, they can be motivational only if employees truly feel as though what they do every day moves them closer—even a little bit closer—to the moon. Many people falsely assume that a company that "watches its numbers" all the time must be controlling and not open to an empowerment mind-set. But in fact the opposite is true. The numbers allow us all to see what needs doing. Our empowerment strategy supports us as we engage toward achieving our goals.

Ultimately, it's the combination of empowerment and metrics that creates the platform for success. Many companies fear an empowered workplace. They worry that it will devolve into chaos, or that employees will take advantage of the freedom and slack off. But it's my experience that only the empowered workplace effectively attracts and retains top talent. Money is not everything. Many of the most talented individuals in the workplace today want more than just a paycheck—even if it is a substantial paycheck. They want to be valued and trusted. When we tell them, "Go out and do your best work and collaborate with your colleagues to produce amazing results," they are inspired. And when they succeed, we feel the same way we did when we saw the rice merchant's business thrive: proud to have supported and enabled that success.

## EMPOWERING YOURSELF

We tend to think of empowerment as a gift granted to us by others. Your supervisor empowers you to make decisions; your government empowers you to vote; a business empowers you to customize a product. These are all examples of empowerment, to be sure, but they are not the only ways we can experience it. One of my most formative experiences, in both life and work, was the moment I empowered myself.

I was in my thirties and working for the Industrial Bank of Japan. This was a good job. It was a prestigious job. It was a status I had worked hard to achieve by studying in school and applying myself with focus and energy. But I made a decision to leave my position and start my own company. It was not a hasty decision. I had considered my career options and the path I wanted to travel for some time. Ultimately, I chose the somewhat unusual path of entrepreneurship. In Japan, that's not the norm for those with a good university education. The traditional path is to secure an entry-level job at a reputable company and then work hard to move up through the ranks over the course of a lifetime. I could have done that. That option was available to me. I instead made the choice to strike out on my own.

This was a private decision. There was no one telling me to do this. In fact, many advised me to stay at IBJ and stop this silly talk about entrepreneurship. There was not a lot of societal support for my decision. As I've said, the tradition in Japan is to align one's career goals with a company's and make that your career path. So I had to empower myself. I had to decide that this was the way for me, even if I was not showered with support. I would remain focused on my own goal, no matter what.

Empowering oneself is actually harder than empowering someone else. Often, you have to work against many of the traditions and rules you have learned along the way in order to free your own thinking and set audacious goals.

The first step in empowering yourself is to expand your mind. Before you act in an empowered manner, you must be able to think in an empowered manner. Often, this means learning to let your mind roam beyond the parameters of what you have learned in school or been trained to do on the job. Opening your mind to the possible is a skill that must be constantly practiced.

This is another perk of Englishnization. Although it was born as a business communications strategy, it is also an empowerment strategy—one that I experienced and that I want my employees to experience as well. When I insisted that everyone learn to communicate in English, I put them all on a path to thinking outside the boundaries of the Japanese language. When you open your mind to another language, you open your intellectual experience to other cultures, to other ways of doing business. When you can use language to connect across borders, you can communicate on a new level with a wider range of people. Learning a new language frees you from whatever constraints your native language may have and empowers you to make global connections and learn from other traditions. This was certainly my experience as I perfected my English skills, and it is the force that propels me to consider learning additional languages such as Chinese. I recognize how integral language has been to my success.

Another way to empower oneself is to study abroad. Although I had long wished to challenge the rules of traditional Japanese business, my experiences in the Harvard MBA program fanned the flames and gave me the tools and inspiration to carry out my plans.

The most significant part of my study at Harvard did not take place in the classroom. During my time in the United States, I was exposed directly to the entrepreneurial culture that is so widespread there. Harvard Business School was a place where a future generation of economic leaders had come to learn. And what I learned is that it didn't matter how big your company is; what mattered was how much value you create yourself. This concept—a focus on what you, the individual, had created in a business context—was powerfully new to me. I looked around me, and it was clear that this was true well beyond the borders of Harvard. In many cases, people who earned respect in the United States were those who created something and—most significantly to me—acted on their own initiative. Admired individuals were often those who had started their own companies.

This is exactly the opposite of how success is viewed in Japan. My exposure to this competing vision of success radically changed my thinking. My educational experience was fueling my plan of self-empowerment.

And this, in turn, sparked my decision to become an entrepreneur—even in the face of advice to the contrary, even though many around me considered it strange. I had seized the ability to see beyond limited traditions and expectations. I had created in myself a wider spectrum of possibilities. No one could have given this to me. I had to discover it and embrace it for myself.

## EMPOWERING THE WORLD

There is still much more opportunity for empowerment around the world, and I believe business—especially e-commerce—can lead the way.

Soon after I left IBJ to follow my entrepreneurial calling, I converted my first recruit. I met one day with a young man named Shinnosuke Honjo. He was an alumnus of a top university in Japan, and he was eager to secure a position at IBJ. He had read everything that had been published about the bank, and he was now conducting informational interviews about IBJ in hopes of becoming the ideal candidate for a job there. He was 100 percent focused on securing the life of a traditional Japanese salaryman at a traditional Japanese company. The word "empowerment" was nowhere in his lexicon.

But when I met with him, I heard something interesting in his conversation. I asked him why he wanted to join IBJ, and he answered me saying, "I want to be of some service to the creation of new corporations and new industries."

I told him the thought I had been turning over in my own mind: "The days when banks and trading companies and other large corporations can change Japan and build our society have come to an end. Nowadays, it is rather individuals, and small and medium enterprises, that will steadily create new ideas and create change in Japan."

By the end of my conversation with Honjo, I had persuaded him to stop trying to work for IBJ and instead to come work for me. It was the next step in my devotion to empowerment: empowering others.

As I spoke with Honjo, I was still deciding what I would do next with my career. I had left IBJ and gone out on my own, so my process of self-empowerment was well under way. But in those first years, I ran a consulting business, assisting companies involved in mergers and acquisitions. I was still searching for the idea that would serve as the foundation for my company.

As I searched, I began to think more broadly about where my interest in empowerment would take me. I was slowly realizing it was much bigger than my own personal ambitions, or even the ambitions of the company I would start and run. Empowerment, I decided, was a national and even a global strategy.

## THE LESSON OF THE PIRATES

To understand how empowerment will change the world, consider this question: Why are there so few pirates today?

There was a time when piracy was far more prevalent. In fact, in ages past, pirates were a kind of merchant. With each adversary they faced, they had to make a decision: plunder or bargain. If it was more profitable to plunder, they plundered. If it was more profitable to enter in a deal with opposing party, they made a deal. It was strictly a business decision. Even plundering had its costs.

Pirates flourished when the world was large, and they had lots of space to roam freely and without consequence. But as communications improved and the world became "small," plundering became a lot more costly and bargaining more appealing.

Today, the Internet is making that small world even smaller, and bargaining ever more essential. Today, when you meet an adversary on the field of business, you can grab your opportunity, or you can look for a way to create a win-win situation. At the heart of a win-win arrangement is the concept of empowerment. When only one side controls the process, only one side can profit. When both sides are empowered, both emerge as winners.

We see this over and over in our e-commerce business. When we empower our customers, they want to continue the process and spread the win-win message. One of our merchants is a chocolate maker who calls his business Vanilla Beans. He launched more than a decade ago. He faced challenges in his early years: how to ship delicately made chocolate treats so that they didn't break in transit; how to move chocolates safely during the hot summer months; and how to find great new trends in candy and incorporate them into his own line of now thirty different products.

But even as he pursues his business, he himself is an ambassador of the Rakuten empowerment message. "We want everyone to be happy," says owner Katsuhisa Yagi. "The people who grow the chocolate, the people who make it, the people who eat it." Since 2009, Yagi has sourced his materials from the Ivory Coast and Ghana in accordance with fair-trade policies. Every week, his company auctions off any misshapen chocolate pieces that came off the production line and 90 percent of the proceeds go toward building a school in Ghana. His company motto is "Making the world happy with chocolate." Not just his customers, but the world. And Rakuten encourages him and gives him a way to do that.

Today, old traditions of piracy are on the wane. Our interconnected world demands more accountability; plunderers now face consequences. This fuels the undercurrent of empowerment that I see in myself, in my company, and in the global business world. The future leaders will not be the plunderers who grab and dominate. They will be those at companies that empower and negotiate.

Empowerment is a way to make customers happy. Empowerment is way to inspire employees to do their best work. Empowerment is a way to look within and discover your own best potential. And empowerment is the engine that will drive creativity and prosperity in the ever-shrinking world.

## TRY THE RAKUTEN WAY

To incorporate a spirit of empowerment into your business, consider these steps:

- Empower yourself first. Recognize that you have the power and the responsibility to make decisions for yourself. Act on your decisions and embrace them. Do not allow events to carry you along. Be active in your efforts and not passive. You will be better able to lead an empowerment strategy if you can do so from firsthand experience.
- Make empowerment part of a strategic plan, not a "soft" goal. Make empowerment a "must have" rather than a "nice to have" element in your business.
- Measure the results. This will help inspire everyone to pursue the empowerment strategy and it will guard against a chaotic work environment.

# THREE

# REWRITING THE RULES OF EXPANSION

## GOING GLOBAL

There is a concept in Japanese culture we call Galápagos syndrome. It is a term that describes the process of a product or a society evolving in isolation from globalization. The phrase is a reference to a similar phenomenon observed in the Galápagos Islands, and described by Charles Darwin, where plants and animals evolved in isolation from other locations.

Japan today wrestles with the effects of its own Galápagos syndrome. We are an island nation, and the cultural impact of this fact is very present in our language and our business practices. Yet it is critical that we evolve beyond that island thinking and connect with the global community. It is necessary both for the success of our businesses in Japan and for the success of our society as a whole. For a while, the economy of our island was large enough to sustain us. But we are reaching the limit of what our island can provide. Globalization is our critical next move.

Japan is not the only nation facing this reality. Globalization is a necessary step for nations all over the world. For some, the impetus is similar to Japan—the need to reach out for new markets and new ideas. Others need to connect with resources not available in their own country. But no nation can afford to remain isolated. Any company—any country—attempting to sit this development out will simply be left behind. When I first began the process of taking Rakuten global, I was asked by more than one Japanese reporter: Why are you going global?

I had to laugh when I heard this. I told each reporter, "If you were an American or European reporter, you would be asking me, 'Why has it taken you so long to go global?'"

I make globalization a priority because Japan and Japanese companies have so much to lose if they fail to go global. At the same time, I recognize that globalization will do much more than improve my company's financial fortunes. It will be the underpinning of the new world economic system. From my perspective, globalization is like English—it is the common state of the world business community, just as English has become its common language.

Yet for such a critical process, many companies execute it poorly. Globalization is not just about sending out sales reps to faraway lands. It is a process that must be ingrained in the corporate culture and applied to the broader corporate goals. Too often, companies look at an international expansion as a sideshow—an offshoot of the company's "real" mission. Those who look at globalization as a hobby will inevitably fail to execute it properly. In this chapter, I'll discuss my globalization strategy. I will review:

- The importance of a global mind-set
- The creation of a global product
- The execution of a global marketing strategy
- My "federation" versus "imperial" process for managing global divisions
- The steps toward creating a global human resources strategy

## DEVELOPING A GLOBAL MIND-SET

The process of globalization does not begin with international travel. It begins in your home office, at your desk, as you position yourself mentally to consider the world as part of your business plan.

For many, this is a challenge. It is not solely a Japanese tendency to be more comfortable in one's own domestic market than in the broader global community. What's more, that hesitancy is well placed. If you make a mistake in an international effort, the results can be costly and can hurt your company's reputation. So wandering across international borders without preparation is not advisable either. Globalization must be carried out from a place of considered planning. This begins with a preparation of the mind.

## GET YOUR NEWS FROM THE WORLD

Your first step in globalization must be to reach out to the world for information. Any local news source will naturally be focused on the themes and demands of its local market. This is very true in Japan, where local media are focused on "scoops" and are less attentive to considered opinions and commentary. This is very different from the media landscape in the United States and Europe, where opinion and commentary are common.

But all local media have their limitations. To understand the world, you must be willing to consume foreign media regularly. Even if you are not well versed in a particular language, get a dictionary and plow through. You will find it is worthwhile. Getting news from outside your domestic market will not only give you the concrete facts you may need to do business there, it will expose you to larger themes and social trends that may affect your business. You can't rely on your own country's media to do this job for you.

When reading the news of the world, focus not only on the facts that may aid your business, but also on ideas that may apply to you in more creative ways. Reading the news of another country may expose you to new ways of thinking, new concepts, and new angles. While they may not be immediately useful in your business, opening your mind to new possibilities will ready it for when that game-changing information does come along. This is a critical element of the global mind-set—the ability to perceive and experience ideas from other cultures.

## GET YOUR FACTS FROM THE WORLD

Reading the world's news is good, but not enough to solidify the global mind-set. A newspaper—even a great newspaper—is still secondary information. My advice is to be sure you supplement your news with primary-source information. If you are in the food business, make an effort to seek out primary sources such as farmers and retailers. They are on the ground in the marketplace, and their information is unfiltered and often illuminating. Don't just assume newspaper reports have given you everything you need to know about a consumer trend. Make an effort to connect with end users—talk to customers about their experiences.

In short, create your own news network. Reach out to new sources of data and incorporate them into your own personal media feed. Reach outside your own personal information circle to learn about the world beyond your borders.

As part of this process, I recommend travel. There is no better way to gather facts about a place than to travel there and do the work yourself. The great intellectuals of the Meiji Restoration in the mid-1800s lived in an era when the only method of international travel was a long and dangerous journey by sea. Yet they traveled to the United States and to Europe to see with their own eyes and hear with their own ears about the modern civilizations there. The experiences and inspirations harvested from these journeys became a driving force for Japan's progress during that period.

Did they have to undertake that arduous travel? There were certainly many books from Europe and the United States at the time, as well as people who visited Japan from those regions. The intellectuals of that era could have simply read the books and listened to the stories of their foreign visitors. But they knew this was not enough. They knew that you can never really understand a place and learn all it has to teach from secondary sources. There is an impact and an immediacy that come from firsthand experience that can't be transferred.

I have had this experience many times in my work. Today, I make two international trips every month. This puts me on the road (and in the air) quite a bit. It makes running my company complicated, since I am often in different time zones from my Tokyo-based team. It takes me away from my wife and children. So traveling can be hard on the many other things I want to accomplish in my life.

Still, I know travel is essential to maintaining a global mind-set and driving globalization throughout my business. There are experiences that take place in my travels that I could not have back in my office in Tokyo. Once, while on a short trip to Spain, I had a free hour, so I walked around a marketplace in Barcelona. It was a tremendous sensory experience—seeing the colors of the goods for sale, feeling the energy of the merchants and the shoppers, hearing the chatter of commerce around me. I was struck as I walked through the marketplace with how exciting it was to be there. And it started me thinking: What can we do to create this level of excitement in our online marketplace? What can we do to give the virtual customer the energy and sensory pleasure of what goes on here? This kind of inspiration is not something I could have had back home. Had I been back in Tokyo that morning, I might have logged on to the Rakuten marketplace and decided, *Looks good. Nothing new needed here.* But when I traveled and experienced the Barcelona marketplace, my mind was opened to new possibilities. This is primary information I took back with me and began applying to our web design and retail environment teams.

## STUDY THE WORLD'S SUCCESS STORIES

Why are some companies so successful? To be successful in the global marketplace, you must study the global leaders.

Too often I find that people do not pay attention to the success stories on the global stage. They may understand in great detail why a company succeeds locally, but they are less able to articulate why some firms are successful on a global scale. To my thinking, this is the obvious question for our time. Perhaps it is easier to understand why a company is successful locally and more complicated to understand reasons for global success. But these are the big questions we must address.

It is not simply a question of good luck. There are reasons why some companies are the world's best. You should make an effort to understand these reasons and look for ways to apply what you learn to your own business. The benefits of global thinking include not just the opportunity to make money in the global marketplace, but also to learn from the leaders in the global marketplace. Here are three things they do well:

## DEVELOP A GLOBAL PRODUCT

Let's go back once more to the reporters who questioned my decision to expand into the global marketplace. Why go global?

Certainly, the first reason is because you need new markets in order to grow. But another important reason is this: I knew I had a global product.

Some may fail to see how a company like Rakuten has a "product." We are not a manufacturer. We are not like Toyota or Mitsubishi. We do not have factories and we do not produce an item you can touch and feel. Yet we do have a product, one that we export to the global marketplace. That product is my organization.

When Rakuten goes into a new market, it brings two key strengths. One is the technology platform that we have developed. The other is the system of management that we have created to leverage and run this technology platform. Together, these form the Rakuten product.

The Rakuten technology platform is a priority I have known was important from the very start of our company. In the early days of Rakuten, we had just one server. It was a machine I personally went down to Akihabara (the technology retail district in Tokyo) to buy and carry back to the office myself. Humble beginnings!

Today, that first server sits in a glass case in the lobby of the headquarters—a reminder of where we started. Now we have data centers throughout Japan, and each can accommodate thousands of servers. One data center alone can fill an office building. I am often struck when I enter one of these data centers, with its cool temperatures and the hum of machines, that this is just a small section of the vast Internet. As our technology platform grew, it was clear that this was an asset we could and should leverage in new markets. When we travel to new counties, we talk about the possibilities that the Rakuten platform can bring, such as expansion into new markets around the world. We explain how we've developed it to maximize empowerment of the user, allowing the merchant to customize a site and engage directly with the customer. Empowerment is a globally understood concept—making our technology a global product with global appeal.

This was our process when we entered new markets. In Indonesia, we were able to find a partner and launch a joint venture. In Malaysia, we started from a "green field"—and built the business from scratch. In both instances, our technology allowed us to create and grow new business opportunities for our own company and for our new partners and customers.

Because we look at our technology as a product, we apply many of the strategies of the great manufacturers. For example, Toyota was famous for its application of *kaizen,* or constant improvement. This is a philosophy that allowed it to produce better and better cars, never resting on any one plateau of success. We look at our technology in the same way. While it is a successful product for us now, it will also require constant maintenance to stay that way. The concept of kaizen is perhaps even more crucial in the Internet business than in automobile manufacturing, given the speed with which the Internet changes and evolves.

To keep our technology in a constant state of improvement, I launched a division of the company called the Rakuten Institute of Technology. This collection of fifty engineers, designers, and computer specialists is charged with the task of coming up with the innovations that will propel our company, our industry, and our customers forward. In many ways, RIT is the fire under the feet of our technology. Even as our technology is helping us achieve new success, the ideas coming out of RIT are saying clearly: More can be done. There is room for improvement. While RIT clusters are located in Tokyo, New York, and San Francisco, staffers are recruited from all over the world. We have also opened R&D centers in several international markets in order to tap into the ideas and wisdom that may be bubbling up there.

But the Rakuten product is not technology alone. Our management system is the equally important yin to the technological yang. Like our technology, the human organization we created was planned from day one. It was a carefully considered process, and absolutely critical to our success. This is the framework I call *Rakuten Shugi*—the Rakuten Way. It is embodied in the Five Principles for Success: Always Improve, Always Advance; Passionately Professional; Hypothesize → Practice → Validate → *Shikumika* (Systemize); Maximize Customer Satisfaction; and Speed!! Speed!! Speed!! I will delve into these five principles in greater detail in my chapter on corporate culture. But I will say here that these five principles and their guiding force in our organization are a key element in our global success. As we venture into new markets, we go with our cutting-edge technology and our strong corporate organization—a strong sense of who we are and how we want to do business. This allows us to present an attractive product to global partners. Our product is our organization. And we are finding eager customers all over the world.

To the reporters who questioned me: This is why we go global. Because we have a global product—an organization powered by always improving technology and empowered human systems—that can bring Rakuten's brand of success to new international marketplaces.

## CREATE A GLOBAL MARKETING PROGRAM

If you have a global product, you need a global marketing effort. It is time-consuming and ultimately self-defeating to reinvent your marketing message in each country you enter. Yet finding a theme that works on a global level is a challenge.

To address this challenge, it's important not to get too distracted by the details of your product, and to stay focused on the human reasons customers buy from you. What is the connection your product makes with customers? Ultimately, this must be the source of your marketing strategy. At Rakuten, we launched our first major global marketing effort under the theme that first made us popular with tiny merchants all over Japan: service.

This requires some explanation, since the kind of service I am describing is not often what others think of when they hear the word. I am not talking about the basic elements of customer service—providing a good product at a fair price, executing the sale seamlessly, etc. These are necessary to any business, and not a strong enough theme to carry a global marketing program. The type of service to which I am referring has a special name in Japanese. We call it *omotenashi*. It is difficult to translate exactly, but the best English equivalent would be "service mind-set." Omotenashi goes beyond the Western concept of providing a customer with service. Omotenashi is focused more deeply on the mind-set of the service provider. You are not just going through the motions of appropriate customer service; you are putting yourself in a constant-state-of-service mind. You are placing yourself in the service of your customer, not just through the current transaction, but always. It's not a short-term exchange of actions, but an overarching theme of the relationship.

Omotenashi is a prevalent concept in the world of Japanese hospitality. It pervades the tourism industry, our hotels and inns, our restaurants, and our arts institutions. And as Rakuten expands its presence in the global marketplace, it is the mind-set I want to pervade our actions: a theme of ongoing, deeply held, personally committed service. We are not here simply to facilitate e-commerce transactions, but to be in a service mind to our customers on a constant basis.

I make this a theme not just of our actions, but of our marketing. Why? This is the theme with which I want Rakuten to be associated as we expand globally. When we come into a new country, the natural response from the local population is: What is Rakuten? Who is Hiroshi Mikitani? Why should we want to do business with this company? Why should we allow this company to become involved with our economy and our people?

A strong global marketing program should answer those questions. It should communicate to the markets you enter who you are and what you value. When we come to a market with the theme of omotenashi, we say: "We are at your service." This sets us apart from other Internet service providers. When a firm like Amazon enters the marketplace, the marketing promise is about efficiency and speed. Certainly, we also strive to provide efficiency and speed, and appreciate their importance. But it is not the essence of who we are and what we hope to accomplish in our relationships in new global markets. Omotenashi is not an easy concept to translate and explain. But it is the core theme of our marketing efforts as we move beyond Japan. It is the answer to the question "Who is Rakuten?"

## UNDERSTAND THE CHOICE:
## FEDERATION VERSUS IMPERIALISM

Going global is not just about entering a marketplace; it is also about doing business once you are there. Rakuten has a unique strategy for doing business in the global marketplace. It stems from our concept of empowerment. We take what I like to call a "federation" strategy as opposed to an "imperial" strategy. This choice, we believe, creates the basis for long-term success.

Many firms move into a new international market by making an acquisition (which we certainly have done, and our acquisition process is well detailed in another chapter). But what happens after the acquisition? Many companies take an imperial stance with the acquired firm. They may send in executives from the home office to run the show. They may discontinue all the old relationships the company had with its local vendors and then start over. In short, they may seek to replicate the original firm in the new country.

This process, to my mind, ignores many potential benefits, and in fact incurs a host of new risks. The way I come into a new market is with the knowledge that empowerment and partnership built Rakuten, a theme that should carry us forward into the global market. When we make an acquisition, we enter the new firm with an eye toward collaboration. What can we do together that will improve the fortunes of all? This was the process we followed when we entered the U.S. market with the acquisition of Buy.com (now Rakuten .com). Our goal in that purchase was not to take over, but to foster new collaborative relationships with the Buy.com network. Like Rakuten in Japan, Buy.com draws its power from a wide marketplace of small and midsize businesses. At the first merchants' conference after the acquisition, we looked to science fiction to try to explain our intentions. The opening presentation of the conference featured a cartoon titled "Federation versus the Death Star" (with Rakuten cast as the Federation and our competition as the Death Star). Everyone laughed, but the message was serious. It underscored our process and our goals. We are not expanding with an eye toward global takeover. We see expansion as an opportunity to foster greater empowerment for all, to deliver our brand of omotenashi in a new environment. Granted, a federation is sometimes harder to run. It might be simpler to be more imperial in our global process. But such a stance would go against the core mission of Rakuten. We began life as a process for empowerment. Now we take that mission into global markets.

When we go into a market with a collaborative spirit, we find that we learn as much as we teach. Often an experience in one international market will show us how to solve a larger problem in the e-commerce system. For example, when we began doing business in Indonesia, we found that customers were hesitant to enter their credit card numbers online. An aura of mistrust, and a fear of fraud, still hung over e-commerce in that country. We could tell that the customers wanted to do business with us—they would visit our site and put items into the virtual shopping cart. But often they would abandon the purchase. It was suggested to us by a local team member that we try a pay-on-delivery system. We equipped teams of moped-riding deliverymen with handheld devices and sent them out to customers' homes and businesses. Customers made the initial selection of an item online, and then we sent the deliveryman out to finalize the transaction in person. Customers could make the purchase without the fear of entering a credit card online.

This seemed a little crazy to us at first, but it succeeded. The pay-on-delivery system worked, and it encouraged this new market of customers to trust us and do business with us. We were willing to literally go the extra mile to serve them. And in the end, it did far more than help our business in Indonesia. It offered us a new process that we may now be able to adapt to the many other international markets where fear of Internet shopping is still an issue. We learned something from our global partner. When you go in with an "imperial" attitude, you assume you know it all and have nothing new to learn. When you go in with the idea of creating a federation, you are often surprised by just how much your new partners can teach you.

## DEVELOP GLOBAL HR

In the earliest days of my company, managing human resources was relatively easy. My first team was made up of six men—all Japanese, all younger than I was at the time, and all schooled in the same systems of hierarchy and performance as I had been. We were a very homogeneous group, and as a result, managing the human needs of this group that so closely reflected my own experience was relatively simple. I could rely exclusively on my own pattern, my own goals, and my own needs as an HR guide.

This similarity of background certainly simplified my efforts. When I told this early group that we were close to a deadline and therefore everyone had to devote all their time and effort to our project—even if that meant sleeping in the office—I encountered little resistance. This was a crew that understood the cultural underpinning of my orders. We had all grown up in the same society and had a similar worldview.

Of course, as the company grew, managing the people involved became more complicated. And as Rakuten pursues a strategy of becoming a fully global company, it will only become more complex in the years to come. Today's Rakuten could not be more different from the band of six I led back in the early days. Today, we have e-commerce operations in thirteen countries and regions including Japan, and nineteen countries and regions including all the services and businesses. We employ more than ten thousand individuals (including contract employees and part-timers) from more than thirty different countries, and our goal is to increase the diversity of our firm even further. Today's Rakuten has 14 percent of its head count from countries other than Japan. It is my goal to bring that percentage up to 39 percent in the next few years. This is the way I intend to make Rakuten a truly global firm—by diversifying both the countries we work in and the people we employ. Being global is not just about where you are located but also whom you employ. A global company naturally needs a global workforce.

That said, when you have a global workforce, you need to tend to that workforce in a way that both supports the company goals and the diversity of the employees within it. As the world becomes more connected and national borders no longer restrict the ways in which people work, the need to develop a truly global HR process will be the priority of successful companies all around the world. The age in which homogeneous staffs did business within their own cultural bubble is rapidly fading.

## FIRST STEP: CHOOSING A DIRECTION

I gathered my executive officers at a retreat to discuss the need for a global HR strategy and the options that were before us. At the time, we were operating on a bit of a patchwork system. We had an overarching human resources department at our headquarters in Japan. But we also had within our system the HR departments of all the companies we had acquired—and this was getting to be a rather long list. We had legacy HR offices in the United States, the United Kingdom, Germany, France, Taiwan, and Thailand, just to name a few. Every time we absorbed a new company, its HR department came right along with it.

We did not want to disrupt the functioning of these acquired companies by simply shutting down the system that had managed the needs and requirements of the human workforce. After all, their HR departments provided vital functions in delivering benefits, maintaining a recruiting and training schedule, and dealing with the everyday work issues of promotions, raises, and handling problem employees. At the same time, we could not simply let each acquired company continue to operate an HR system outside the broader Rakuten chain of command. Becoming part of the Rakuten universe involves more than just acquiring a financial status. We needed to leverage HR to deliver not just Rakuten work policies, but also Rakuten vision and Rakuten Shugi. This was critical to our becoming a unified company and not just a collection of individual offices all over the world. So designing a functioning global HR system was critical. We were big and diverse and only planning to become more so. The time for action had come.

As we reviewed the landscape, we considered the paths carved by multinationals before us. Certainly, there are many firms doing business all over the world that have developed a range of different HR systems to manage this diversity. Three primary systems were evident in the marketplace:

## Type A: Centralization

This is the system of human resources used by many companies. Apple is one example. It retains a tight hold within the company's nation of origin and relies on high-level headquarters staff to supervise local managers. The system is organized with global executives at the top of the pyramid. Below that first layer, you find a group of headquarters managers and beside them a group of local managers—managers stationed in the various non-HQ counties. The headquarters managers are responsible for the headquarters staff and the local managers supervise the local staff. Both local and HQ teams report to the global executive.

The benefit of this system is that it maintains strict brand control. Products are standardized within regions. The strategy is one of export. Products and behavior are all controlled by headquarters. When you think of a company like Apple, it's not hard to see how this system of global organization works. Apple's products are the same all over the world. Whether you buy your iPhone in New York or Tokyo or Rio, it looks and works the same. Apple does not just maintain this sameness in product—it is a theme that runs throughout its global operations. Stores all over the world look the same. Employees all over the world wear the same uniform, receive the same training, and sell the same products. Indeed, Apple strictly polices any attempt by resellers to break off from the Apple way. Apple's brand is tied closely to this uniform execution, and the company often will not do business in a marketplace where it cannot maintain this level of control.

Amazon also adheres to this one-company, one-system method of global operations. No matter where in the world you open an Amazon page, it will have the look and organization that Amazon has made its trademark. As a vendor, no matter where in the world you are or what it is you sell, you will be governed by the rules set by Amazon's headquarters.

No doubt this system works well for companies like Amazon and Apple, but it was not for Rakuten. In the centralized system, everyone is managed by the top-level global executives, but there is no mixing of the lower ranks; headquarters operates parallel to, but not in conjunction with, the staffs in other countries. It may serve to maintain a strict brand identity, but it does not allow for the kind of collaboration we want to promote in the Rakuten system. We did not expand into other countries just to sell into those marketplaces. We did so to learn from the best practices there and to share knowledge and efforts. What's more, the top-down system leaves little room for the empowerment process we value as a company. For all these reasons, centralization is not for us.

## Type B: Localization

This global operating system goes to the opposite extreme. In a localized system, the product strategy varies by location. The global development strategy is also local and self-supporting. Decisions are made at the local country level and designed to deal with local issues directly. In fact, the only issues controlled by headquarters in the country of origin are financial. Everything else falls to local executives, local managers, and local staff.

This pyramid type of global operation has very little room for integration. Only the very top level of the company—the highest executive offices—would have an integrated system in which leaders from all countries might be tapped to come to HQ and serve. But everything below the executive level is entirely drawn and situated in the diverse counties. McDonald's, for example, follows this system of global operations. Back in the United States, there are executives charged with managing the efforts of McDonald's operations around the world. Everything below that one executive level is more local: In China, for example, McDonald's employs a local executive, local managers, and local staff. It stocks products based both on the familiar U.S. menu and on local tastes (for instance, it offers red-bean sundaes). It develops strategies to deal with customers and employees locally, with a goal of managing its distinct area of the world and little effort to export any knowledge or practices to other McDonald's locations around the world. For example, McDonald's in Cairo has had great success using delivery by moped. This fits in well with the popular local custom of fast, individual delivery. But there is little push to bring the moped delivery system to other locations.

While the localization strategy certainly appeals to us in its support of local empowerment, the lack of integration throughout the management hierarchy remains a problem. While we embrace and support empowerment, Rakuten has a core set of values, goals and processes that we are unwilling to give up as we go global. A fully localized operating system made it too likely that everything we had developed in Japan—our culture, our systems, and our vision—would remain there. The companies we acquired would be cut off from the mission we had developed at headquarters.

## Type C: Hybrid

The answer, therefore, was to adopt a hybrid of these systems—a combination of centralized authority and local empowerment. With two ideologies entwined, we could create a system that managed our growing diversity. In the hybrid system, the global executive and global manager ranks are fully integrated—drawing from all locations. We would need a strong system of training and promotion to ensure that managers from all our locations would have the opportunity to rise through their local ranks to move into the integrated manager and executive ranks. These leaders would then be responsible for managing local staff.

In this hybrid system, product strategy is localized and driven by the needs of the local customer base. However, global development strategy is not walled off in the local area, but instead it is connected to a multilateral networking system. In this way, great ideas in one location can spread. When we learned that security concerns in Indonesia could be overcome by sending a staffer out on a moped to conduct the final credit card swipe and final transaction, we set about re-creating that process in other Asian countries where similar security concerns have acted as a damper on e-commerce sales. A solution in one location can be a solution in many— the mandate to HR is to create a system in which employees can connect, share, and network easily and with the support of management.

This hybrid system is one that we see in action across many successful multinationals. IBM and Panasonic have made it famous in technology. Proctor & Gamble and Nestlé have adopted it to develop and market consumer products around the world. In many ways, this system made the most sense for Rakuten.

But even as we zeroed in on the framework we wanted, we were not ready to simply adopt the outline used by others.

As much as we could learn from these other companies, Rakuten was operating in a new, connected world. As companies like Panasonic and P&G grew up decades ago, they did not need to contend with the impact of digital communication, borderless commerce, and globalized markets. So while we saw these firms as a starting point, it was clear to us that we would still need to develop a system that would take the best of this hybrid arrangement and layer on top of it the processes and systems that would allow us to thrive in the fast-moving Internet marketplace.

## STEP TWO: CREATE A PATH FOR MANAGERS

One of our biggest early challenges was how to train and promote managers. As we grew in Japan, naturally our promotion path flowed through our Japanese headquarters. But if we were to be a truly global organization, this could not continue. We needed to find a way to globalize the managerial career path.

It began in recruiting. We integrated the recruiting process into our Englishnization process. We wanted to attract a certain type of individual to our management training process, and English played a key role in this effort. One senior manager who often deals with new recruits spoke about the need to attract aggressive, ambitious new recruits—"meat eaters," as he called them. These are people with a go-getter attitude, a desire to strike first and not be timid. English, that manager says, helps him attract these "meat eaters."

"It's very much embedded in the way the two languages work," he explained. English, he says, is a very direct and specific language. The nature of the Japanese language, on the other hand, leads the speaker to be indirect, less aggressive, and more circumspect.

"That may be very good in literature or philosophy, but in business, the more direct speaking style is better," my manager says. For this reason, English has helped my manager attract those who are direct and aggressive, weeding out the less ambitious types.

From there, we set up two career tracks to help us achieve our goal of integrated global management and executive ranks.

For non-Japanese recruits and those who were Japanese but already bilingual, we developed a two- or three-year assignment within Japan Ichiba—the Japan-based e-commerce business, the first and most developed of Rakuten's divisions. This is our headquarters assignment, where recruits would come to absorb the central themes of Rakuten's business and the many pieces of the Rakuten puzzle that come together in the headquarters environment.

Following this headquarters assignment, successful members of this pool of recruits would be ready for a global assignment. They might move directly into an assignment or into the Global Resource Pool for future assignment. Today, that assignment could be located in any one of more than a dozen countries—and we are adding new global markets at a rapid pace. The possibilities are many for these recruits who come to us with already-developed global business skills. By virtue of their bilingual language skills or their experiences living outside their country of origin, these recruits are often quickly able to embrace the Rakuten way and then implement it in global assignments. This is an increasingly important part of our recruiting and management training process.

Alongside this track, we created another system for our Japanese-born recruits. Although our goal is to be a thriving global company, our roots are still in Japan and the majority of our workforce were born and raised in Japan. This is a workforce we must also train for the global experience. This group travels from recruitment into a Japan Ichiba assignment—but one perhaps shorter than the non-Japanese group's. We estimate that successful Japanese recruits may spend one to two years in this assignment. From there, we move them into our Global Experience Program. This six-month training program is designed specifically to transition Japanese workers— who perhaps were never schooled to consider work outside Japan—to embrace the path of global experience. The results of this GEP vary by recruit. Some finish this program and are ready for a global assignment; they may move into the assignment right away, into the Global Resource Pool for a future assignment, or into another stint at Japan Ichiba where their combination of native Japanese skills is combined with a global education training background.

Our dual tracks for managers is one way our HR system both acknowledges the challenges we face and keeps the goals of the company at the forefront of HR policy. Certainly, as we recruit from around the world, we will have to cope with the fact that our diverse workforce will come to us with diverse languages, diverse cultural expectations, and diverse skills. We can't simply assume that one size fits all when it comes to recruits. That would simply ignore the reality of our situation.

At the same time, we can't have a different training system for every country in which we do business. That would quickly become unwieldy. But most importantly, too many training tracks leave too much opportunity for the core culture of Rakuten to be lost in translation. The culture of our company is the core of our success. It's so important to me that I've devoted a single chapter in this book just to cultural issues. One of my early books in Japanese focused exclusively on the Rakuten culture. With that so fundamental to our success, it is only fitting that our management-training track see cultural training as a core principle.

We are working to build a system of employee exchange as another way to have employees experience both headquarters and the global marketplace. While mostly one-sided at present, Rakuten employees in Japan are sent on assignment to overseas branch companies. In the future, I expect employees will be sent both ways, and there will be a lot more of everybody working together worldwide. Starting last year, directors and capable development-team staff from the United States began coming to Japan on assignment. Tokyo is currently acting as the hub, but I expect that exchanges between other regional headquarters such as those in France or Thailand will soon pick up steam.

Ultimately our system is a combination of classroom and on-the-job training. But it is infused with an element of

Rakuten culture that is quite different from other companies in the marketplace. In addition to learning from teachers and mentors, I expect and encourage Rakuten employees to learn from one another. This requires a level of open discussion in which everyone can participate. As part of teaching one another, I want us to be open with internal information.

I like people who jabber away without concealing anything, and I myself am an open person. As one extreme example of how open we are, even people brand-new to Rakuten Ichiba can access weekly results and trends for our other businesses. Successes from all parts of the company are constantly being shared. This is why I believe that experiencing Rakuten's "secret to success," or, as we like to call it, the "Rakuten Mystery," will be the most important asset in our employees' lives.

## STEP THREE: CREATE A PATH FOR ENGINEERS

As I mentioned, one of the reasons it's not possible to simply copy the HR process of a P&G is the fact that we live in the Internet age, and many of the demands on a company are new. One of those new pressures is the competition any ambitious IT company must engage in to attract and retain top engineering talent. While P&G and other firms have their own recruiting challenges, when I look at Rakuten's HR goals, one of the elements that is always on the top of our list is finding and retaining top engineers. The world does not have enough high-level engineering talent to go around, and companies like Rakuten are on an ongoing talent hunt.

At Rakuten, these collections of workers are called development units. They are critical to our success, as they keep us on the cutting edge of technology. In order to maintain our position at the forefront of new technology, we must find ways to align our technology policy with our HR policy—to ensure that we have the human capital to achieve our technology goals.

We have begun this process by working to develop central tenets for our management of technology and innovation processes. It is our goal to recruit and train so that any of our engineers can work from any of our development units around the world. We are working on ways to centralize some core technologies so that skill sets are applicable across DUs and allow engineers flexibility.

We considered the value of creating a special evaluation and compensation system designed specifically for the engineering talent that we want to attract and retain. As part of this project, we have learned to understand the two levels of compensation the high-level engineer seeks: monetary and non-monetary rewards. Monetary rewards are easy to understand—high-level engineers, like all talented and in-demand individuals around the world, want competitive compensation, long-term incentives, deferred compensation, retirement benefits that reward loyalty, and retention bonuses. That much any company can understand.

But when it comes to non-monetary compensation, the process becomes trickier. There are many things a high-level engineer wants that have nothing to do with money. In fact, the element that is often the most motivational has no currency value: the mission.

Talented engineers want to be recognized for their efforts and contributions. While in the old days engineers toiled behind the scenes, today that is no longer true. Today, a top engineer looks for a career path that will allow him or her to experience the spotlight. And there is also an even more intangible benefit sought by this group: an empathetic connection with top management. Engineers in today's competitive workplace want more than a job; they want a mission. And with that, they want a leader they can believe in. This is not just an HR challenge, but also a leadership challenge. At the CEO level, I must look for ways to communicate my vision to Rakuten staff and help them feel an emotional connection to the battles we face as a company.

Along with that sense of mission, top engineers seek additional elements in a job:

- Career Path: Engineers look for a good initial assignment and for quick and transparent assignments to projects. They don't like to be left hanging, wondering what will happen next. What's more—and perhaps most difficult to deliver—they want to have power. They want to have authority. They do not want to feel as though they are cogs in a machine. To create a career path that embraces these themes is part of our HR challenge.

- Benefits: Not all benefits are monetary. Some are what we would call "soft" benefits, and yet they are of paramount importance to this critical workforce. Talented individuals want to see the company provide benefits not just on an individual level but also on a wider scale, such as by offering an attractive cafeteria on-site, flextime for employees, or a day-care center on the premises. The benefits in this category may even include elements such as casual dress. All come together to create the kind of workplace these engineers want to experience.

We are already starting to see the results of our efforts to retain great engineers, especially when we acquire companies. Though engineers at big firms in the West often quit when the firms are bought out, engineers have for the most part stayed on in Rakuten acquisitions. In the United States and France, for example, there are many truly brilliant engineers. We bring them to Japan or send Japanese employees over there, striving to share best practices.

Understanding the motivations of this critical group of employees is critical to our continued success. If we are not attracting and retaining top engineering talent, all our other efforts will suffer. We are, at the core, a technology company. IT drives who we are and what we can achieve.

It is certainly a challenge to break into new markets, launch new products, generate sales, and increase profits. But as all that is going on, the enormous challenge of recruiting, hiring, and managing people looms. People are not like products. How we deal with our people is often the critical element that lays the groundwork for all the rest of the work the company undertakes. It falls to Rakuten to create a system by which this global orchestra of humanity can learn to work and thrive as one in the digital age. We are never going back to the days I experienced when I first started my company. That homogeneous arrangement can hardly be successful in a world in which everyone—customers, vendors, employees, and managers—can communicate with speed and precision across borders and time zones. A company that tries to manage from a single cultural spot will find itself outpaced by the complex global mind-set that has already taken hold in the Internet age. My loyal band of six would never be able to make a go of it today. That time has passed.

I tell new recruits that joining Rakuten is joining a global company, a firm that will move forward on this broader platform. Global business is not just a way to make money; it is a way to remake the interaction between companies and marketplaces. As these innovations take shape, creating a framework that helps a diverse group of people work together as one will be a critical element to success. Whatever great ideas we have, it will be people who implement them.

## CONCLUSION

Globalization is already a given. The Internet made it so. Once physical barriers to commerce began to fall, the global marketplace appeared. This is true whether a company chooses to participate actively or not. There's no going back to the days of doing business only within one's own borders.

So the questions are: Which companies will be good at it? Which companies will lead the way and provide examples for others to follow? There is much at stake. These models will affect how people all over the world receive goods and services and live their daily lives.

Let me go back and answer the question the reporter asked me—"Why go global now?" Because there are markets all over the world that are ready and eager for our brand of empowerment. We are ready and able to deliver it to them. It is a collaboration whose time has come.

## TRY THE RAKUTEN WAY

- Get your news from the world. Do not be satisfied with local sources. The best new idea may be emerging on the other side of the globe.
- Encourage all employees to consider themselves global employees. Lessons learned locally have applications on the global stage.
- Create career paths that encourage global experience. Make it possible, even preferable, for managers to work outside their countries of origin.

# FOUR

# REWRITING
# THE RULES OF
# ACQUISITION

## BUYING COMPANIES

In the history of Rakuten, we have made dozens of acquisitions. Some were big and drew headlines—such as our acquisition of Kobo, a Canadian maker of eReaders. Some were quite small—tiny firms with interesting new software we wanted to make use of. But big or small, I have a special affection for the acquisition process. I see it not as just a financial strategy, but also a way to find new platforms for my philosophy, new followers, and new inspiration.

Acquisitions are too often assumed to be only a way to make money. Instead, they should be looked at as new chapters in a company's story. They are opportunities to do much more than make money. They are opportunities for everyone involved to rise to a new level of performance.

A senior executive in my company likes to tell this story about my interest in acquisitions: Years ago, when Rakuten was just starting to attract attention within Japan, this executive was at work at his own firm—a company that created and executed loyalty programs. He and I met at a business association function, and he followed up to request a meeting with me to discuss a possible joint venture or other project.

I was not especially interested in a joint venture with his firm, but I did not want to be impolite. After a few months, we found time on my calendar and the meeting took place. We were casually chatting when, suddenly, inspiration struck my visitor. He said, "Would you like to buy my company?"

At that, I sat up, leaned forward, and began to see the meeting in an entirely new light. My visitor noticed this, too. He likes to tell this story by saying, "Then, Mickey's eyes *popped* open."

It had taken my visitor three months to secure a meeting with me; it took him about three weeks to sell his company to Rakuten. He continues to serve as a senior executive officer at Rakuten to this day.

Why do I find acquisitions so interesting? I would say it is because I see so much more than money on the table. An acquisition is an opportunity to take the process of collaboration and empowerment that I so value to its grandest scale. When two companies enter into a merger and acquisition agreement, they are making the most serious commitment to each other that the business world allows. They are agreeing to move forward as one. I know that many in the M&A business see acquisition as the start of a financial strategy—a quick turnaround to make a profit. I view it as a way to begin a long and profitable relationship—between companies, customers, even countries.

In this chapter, I'll explain why I seek out acquisition opportunities and how I go about choosing and executing an acquisition.

## WHY BUY COMPANIES?

The most pressing reason for acquisition is to find new customers. This is a very key reason for Japanese companies, since the Japanese economy alone can no longer support growth. We are a nation with a declining birth rate and, in my own industry, a mature marketplace. It makes sense to expand beyond our national borders in search of additional customers, and acquisitions can be a perfect tool to accomplish this expansion.

Of course, expansion can be achieved simply by opening up branches in new markets, but this is a much slower and more cumbersome process. A smart acquisition buys more than a market—it buys time. When Rakuten makes an acquisition, it enters a marketplace not as a brand-new firm, but as the new owner of an established business. That allows us to immediately begin fostering new growth and making the pie bigger for all—including ourselves, the acquired company, and all the vendors who have been associated with the acquired company. We don't need to spend years laying groundwork and establishing trust; we can do what we do well from the get-go.

This has been our strategy as we've spread from Japan into other parts of Asia, as well as Europe and North America. Our acquisitions in North America are great examples of how we use the process. As we looked to enter the North American marketplace, it was clear that there were already a handful of substantial and established players doing well there—Amazon and eBay, for example. To simply start from scratch in that marketplace would put Rakuten many years behind the leaders in terms of development. Instead, we looked for an acquisition strategy to join this important and flourishing marketplace. We began with LinkShare in 2005. Then we moved on to Buy.com. Then Kobo. All these acquisitions gave us more access to the North American customer and also provided a base to grow the business for all involved. It might be a stretch for a U.S. consumer to check us out by visiting Rakuten Ichiba—perhaps that site was too unknown for the American customer to relate to. But that same customer is comfortable with the well-known Buy.com. And over time, we can introduce that customer to the rest of the Rakuten ecosystem. We gain access to the customer; the Buy.com vendors gain access to the rest of the Rakuten family. Everybody wins.

While acquiring customers is a key strategy, another is acquiring talent. Success in the global marketplace depends heavily on a company's ability to tap into the wide talent market. When we acquire companies, we expand our access to the world's talent supply. When we make a purchase, we usually look for management to stay on. We hope that the talent who created the company we admire will remain to manage it in its next iteration as part of the Rakuten ecosystem. Also, each new acquisition raises the Rakuten profile and makes us more visible to talent outside Japan. The process has been very valuable for us. Recently, as many as half of Rakuten's new hires were non-Japanese. This is part of our strategy to attract and foster a global workforce, and confirms that our acquisition strategy is bringing us more than market assets—it is also bringing us human capital.

Finally, acquiring companies allows us to acquire knowledge. Often when we make an acquisition, we see quickly that we have purchased not just a company, but a set of solutions. When we acquired Paris-based PriceMinister, we learned quickly of the technical solutions they had developed to combat online fraud. This is knowledge and technology we were then able to apply in our efforts to enter other countries. We have many smart people at Rakuten, of course, and an entire division devoted entirely to research and development. But no one can think of everything, and acquisitions often bring with them some great new ideas.

## HOW WE BUY COMPANIES

With all these good reasons propelling us forward, we make frequent acquisitions both in Japan and around the world.

Over time, we have developed a process and institutionalized guidelines. This helps us to be efficient and smart about acquisitions, regardless of where we are buying or the size of the company we are interested in.

Our process has three major points. When we buy a company we look for:

- A long view
- A cultural fit
- Business synergy

I'll go through each one in detail.

## A LONG VIEW

In the broader world of finance, the most profitable acquisitions are usually the quick ones. An acquirer may find a target, make the buy, execute a strategy such as spinning off assets, and exit within a defined period of time. We take a much longer view. When we buy a company, it is a lot like an individual buying a home. Real estate speculators may hop in and out of real estate deals, but a homeowner buys with the intention of staying, raising a family, and becoming part of the community. This is how we view our acquisitions. Profit, while important to us, is not our only goal. We are looking for a "home," whether it is a foothold in a new country or an entry point into a new line of business. Our acquisitions are the opening moves in what we hope and expect will be long, multiyear relationships.

For that reason, we look for partners who share our long-term view. We want to find a company that sees us as a new member of the neighborhood, not as a corporate raider. We look for companies that also take a multiyear outlook, not a chance to "flip" the deal and make a quick profit. We look for management that is thinking about long-term possibilities. This is partially about asking questions, but we also look for evidence of that commitment. For example, has the company fostered long-term relationships with its vendors? Does it care about how long a vendor stays and how happy that vendor is to be part of the corporate network? A company that churns through vendors without worry is not one with which Rakuten will be compatible. That's a company with a short-term profit view. It does not fit with our overall plan.

## A CULTURAL FIT

When we have found a company that suits our business goals and shares our long-term view of the business, we next look for a key factor in any successful collaboration: a cultural fit.

We know that at Rakuten, we do not do business in the same manner as every other company in the marketplace. Rakuten Shugi—the Rakuten Way—is in many aspects unique to us. It is the core of who we are and how we behave every day. There is no element of Rakuten business that does not embrace the Five Principles and does not seek to reflect Rakuten Shugi in everything it does. So when we look for a company to acquire, we discuss the Rakuten Shugi very early on.

Why does this matter so much? Can't a cultural issue be worked out later? Isn't this a "soft" issue, not a core reason to buy or not buy a company? I would argue no. In fact, the cultural fit is so important, it must be discussed long before any financial considerations are on the table. Rakuten Shugi is a huge part of why we are successful. A poor fit with Rakuten culture may indicate other problems ahead.

For example, one element of Rakuten Shugi is our Tuesday-morning tradition in which every employee—from me to the newest member of the staff—cleans his or her own workspace. And when I say "clean," I mean *really* clean. We pick up the trash. We get down on the floor and clean the area under our desks. We polish the legs of our office chairs. Why? Because it is a manifestation of how we care about this company and about the work we do here. If there were trash on the floor of your own home, would you step over it and ignore it? No, of course not; you would make sure on a regular basis that your home was clean and presentable. This is because you care deeply for your home and take pride in its appearance. The Rakuten cleanup taps into that same emotional place. When we clean, and when we put our effort into the process, we show our commitment and our devotion to our mission. This is a process by which we all strive to be modest and push back any tendency to arrogance.

I recognize that this weekly cleanup is uncommon. In fact, I'm not sure I can think of another CEO in another country who polishes his office chair every week. But we hold this particular ritual dear. When we meet with a potential acquisition target, this is one of the cultural discussions we have. Not just about cleaning but more broadly about Rakuten Shugi. We are not looking for obedience or subservience. We are looking for a firm that feels as we do—that the company should be in your heart the same way your home is in your heart, and that everyone should attend to the company with the corresponding attention and devotion.

Another key element of our culture, as we discussed earlier, is empowerment. We seek to empower all members of our ecosystem, and this often contradicts the way many others in the e-commerce industry have built their businesses. Many successful e-commerce companies such as Amazon or Zappos make their living by serving the customer but give far less attention and consideration to the vendor. In our business, we consider vendor empowerment and happiness to be just as important as customer happiness. This is another thing we bring up early when talking to a potential acquisition. If the company's idea of empowerment differs from ours, it may not be a good cultural match.

We are not insisting that the firms we acquire display all the characteristics of Rakuten Shugi. This would be an impossible demand. But we are looking for the right mind-set and a willingness to embrace the Rakuten Shugi. This was certainly the case when we first began talks with Play.com in the United Kingdom. From day one, we were very open with them and they were very open with us; we had many discussions about culture. There were plenty of differences between our operations. But there were also some key cultural "fits."

For example, Play.com was very interested in embracing the notion of empowerment and bringing it to the forefront of its business. Certainly we all understood that change in a culture like the United Kingdom would not be quick or easy. But we could see that with their mind-set inclined toward empowerment, even if it took time we would eventually fit well together.

It is often apparent as early as the first conversation which companies will make successful acquisitions and which will not. The culture discussion reveals whether there is "chemistry" between us. We are not looking for companies that do everything exactly as we do it. But we do want companies that understand *why* we do the things we do—why they have value. Ultimately, an acquired company will need to fit into the Rakuten Shugi. If we can't agree on that, there is no point in talking price.

## BUSINESS SYNERGY

This is the element that is perhaps the most familiar to the business world. Any company, in its dealings with any other, looks for synergy. We look for a synergy between ourselves and the acquired company, and we look for ways we can expand on that synergy post-acquisition.

Synergy is a core motivator of the Rakuten ecosystem. As we have expanded over the years, we have not added business lines that are distant from one another. We have always sought to add lines of business with synergy to our existing divisions. This makes it easy and fluid for a customer of one of our lines to expand their relationship with Rakuten through our other products and services. It is a natural move for a retail customer to then try out our credit card, our travel service, even our investment service.

This is the sort of synergistic experience we seek to replicate when we acquire a company. We look first for a company already in a business that has synergy for us; that is, it's often an e-commerce business of some kind. Then, we look for ways to expand their contributions, bringing them into other elements of our Rakuten ecosystem—introducing their customers to our credit card, our travel services, and our investment services. Finally, we take this new business and introduce it to the global Rakuten customer base. A company that perhaps did business in just one or two countries will now, with our technology platform, maintain a web presence in ten countries. These are all examples of the way synergy is a motivator for us. We look for synergy now, and synergies to come. In this way acquisition can turn one plus one into ten.

One of the best illustrations of this process comes in the story of our finance businesses. While we began our company in e-commerce, many of our first acquisitions were in the field of finance.

When we set about building our financial services businesses, we did so largely through acquisition. We sought out the core companies we thought would add value to our ecosystem and then we brought them into the Rakuten fold, engaged them in the Rakuten process, and integrated them into our broader global corporate system. In each case, the acquisition was designed not just to add to our empire but also to strengthen the businesses we already had in operation. Synergy was our guiding principle at every step.

One of our first forays into the financial world was the acquisition of a credit card business—what would eventually be called Rakuten Card. Nothing so reflects the change in our consumer culture quite like the credit card. It is a plastic symbol of our times. In the early days of credit cards, having one and using one were a big deal. It was reserved for the wealthy and for special purchases. Today, the credit card is as commonplace as cash. We take out our credit cards to buy a cup of coffee or to travel on mass transit. We use it to buy groceries. It is an everyday item.

With the advent of e-commerce, the credit card grew to even greater prominence. Now it is a necessary item to participate in the e-commerce experience. Whether you want to buy a car or download a piece of music, a credit card is part of the transaction.

Once we added a credit card to the business to help facilitate shopping, we then looked to a new area of financial services when we acquired what would become Rakuten Bank. Our goal with this acquisition: to facilitate payments. We made a series of acquisitions that enabled us to provide speed and effective remittance and payment services.

Perhaps there is no greater symbol of the brick-and-mortar era than the bank. For generations, they were the visible manifestation of money and prestige. They anchored Main Streets in small towns and big cities. They were physical monuments to prosperity and power. But while banks have remained important to our lives and our world, their physicality has begun to lose traction. Main Streets have less foot traffic. Individuals and businesses find fewer reasons to go downtown to the bank. Banks still provide necessary services, but they are ensconced in an old-fashioned format—the brick-and-mortar structure. When we entered the banking business, there was no question we would do it in a virtual way. But we also made other important changes to the traditional banking experience.

Bank customers are generally defined by asset volume, but we opted to use a different metric. We measure our customers by their transaction frequency. We focus on the activity of our customers as a signal of how well we are serving their needs and how successful we are at being part of their everyday financial interactions. In the banking business, we applied much of what we had learned in e-commerce. Using an e-commerce business model, we were able to keep our costs low and outperform our competitors.

The key to our financial services divisions is our concept of synergy. As successful as each one might be alone, no Rakuten division operates in a vacuum. As we have added and expanded each of these financial services, we have looked for ways to integrate them into the larger landscape of the Rakuten ecosystem. Many of our new accounts in Rakuten Securities are also members of our loyalty program run via Rakuten Ichiba. Securities customers also earn points that can be used through the loyalty program.

More than just new business ventures, these were all additional ways in which we rewrote the rules. It was unusual at the time for a company like ours to venture into the areas of banking and finance. But this created new ways in which we could offer innovative, lower-cost services to our customers and strengthen the financial position of our own business.

## WHEN AN ACQUISITION FAILS

Despite our success, there have been times when our acquisition strategy has not played out as we expected. One of these was our attempt to purchase Tokyo Broadcasting System.

When I initially approached this idea, it had great synergy possibilities. TBS was an independent broadcast company whose initial business model was under fire. The traditional structure of advertising-supported media was losing steam. So many consumers were able to skip ads by recording shows that the broadcaster could no longer guarantee the "eyeballs" advertisers demanded. This was not unique to TBS or Japanese media by any means—this is the same challenge facing ad-supported media all over the world. Watching it unfold, I began to envision a new construct for media delivery—one that did not depend on the traditional advertising model but instead leveraged the power and reach of the Internet. I figured: If you combine TV with the Internet, it is a home run for all involved. TV gets a new business model, Rakuten gets a new line of business, and consumers get content delivered in a way that suits their lifestyle. This would be a win-win for everyone.

Unfortunately, the leadership of TBS did not share my vision. Rakuten acquired about 20 percent of TBS, and we intended to eventually acquire up to 50 percent. I knew as I went into this deal that it would be a challenge to get TBS to see it my way. But I went into the process confident I could convince TBS leadership of the wisdom of my vision. I knew that many had come up through the ranks of the traditional broadcast business and were wary of the changes taking place in the media world. It seemed to me so clear that the world had been changed by the new technology and companies like TBS would have to change, too. I was fully prepared to put all my effort and support into leading this transformation at TBS. But TBS leadership fought the idea. They did everything they could to block it. They even activated their "poison pill" provision.

What frustrated me most was the way TBS sought to protect its old model rather than embrace what I saw as obvious—the change that the Internet has wrought in the media world. Why would you want to spend all your time and money fighting change that is already under way? Whom does that serve? It frustrated me because it served only to protect those in power, and it did not serve the customer in any meaningful way. The strongest impression I took away from that battle was how stubborn old people could be. But clearly, this was my error. I made the mistake of failing to perceive how resistant to change the leadership of TBS would be.

To be sure, this situation is not unique to TBS, or even Japanese media. Media all over the world have felt the pressure of a changing consumer and changing technology. Some have adapted well, embracing the change; others have fought the change hard, trying to maintain the status quo.

Ultimately I was not successful in making this acquisition happen. After a while, I had to give up. It was not easy. I lost a lot of money—millions of dollars. I was frustrated because it seemed so irrational. But it was a good lesson about cultural fit. I had one vision for the future—one that embraced change and new ideas. TBS leadership had a very different vision for the future—one that protected the old business model and fought off any attempts at change. I went into the acquisition attempt knowing TBS leadership were concerned about this, but I was sure I could convince them. I would persuade them to move on from an outdated business model toward the new possibilities. But I was not able to do this. The cultural fit just wasn't there. I still believe that a media acquisition would be very valuable for Rakuten. I believe that the synergies are there and that the consumer is ready for media to evolve. I just need to find the company that will share my long-term view and my cultural passion for change.

## AFTER THE BUY

Finally, an important part of my strategy for buying companies comes after the company has been purchased—the post-acquisition period. This is perhaps the most critical time in the process, when all parties find out if they were right or wrong about the fellow across the table. The contracts have been signed. The funds have been exchanged. Now the reality of the new ownership sets in.

We consider this an important part of the acquisition process not just because it affects the company we've just purchased, but also because it helps create our image as an acquirer in the global marketplace. Thanks to the Internet, word travels fast. A company acquired in the United States can quickly inform the rest of the world what it's like to be bought by Rakuten. We want those early reports to be positive.

We handle this process in a step-by-step fashion, rolling out ideas and policies in a way that seeks to integrate the new players into the Rakuten team. Our process in Germany provides a good example. We acquired Tradoria, a German e-commerce company, and set about making this new acquisition the basis for Rakuten Deutschland. Our first step was to introduce and teach the concept of Rakuten Shugi to the Tradoria managers and staff. We assigned "homework" to the managers—the reading of my two early books, *Golden Rules of Success* and *Principles for Success*. Once that was complete, we moved to wider group training and had senior officers from Rakuten's Tokyo headquarters come in to conduct Shugi presentations to the full staff. We deployed trainers from our global HR staff to create Shugi training for all newcomers to the company.

As our Shugi training was under way, we worked at the same time to begin the changeover in business processes. We moved tasks such as booking and invoicing over into the Rakuten system. We began implementing a new email system, which is the system used by all Rakuten divisions all over the world. And within months of closing the acquisition, we made the brand shift, rechristening the company Rakuten Deutschland.

These were just our first steps. Of course, the integration of a new acquisition is an ongoing process. But these early steps in which we introduce our corporate culture, our business processes, and our technical tools are key indicators of how we will continue to work on the acquisition even after the ink is dry. Just making the transaction is only part of the process. Making the transaction successful rests on creating the long-term relationships and shared vision that will translate to success for all involved.

## ACQUISITION FOR THE GLOBAL GOOD

Ultimately, to me acquisition is more than a business strategy. It is also part of my vision for a more fully connected world. When companies erase their borders and agree to join forces, they unite in their purpose to serve a common good—the common good of the customer. When acquisitions go well, they enhance the notion that competitors need not always be bitter rivals. When a merger is successful, all parties participate in the success, and this supports the broader idea of global cooperation.

That is why my eyes popped open that day years ago, when my now colleague sat in my office and offered to sell me his company. I saw at that moment a chance not just to do some business, but also to do some good.

## TRY THE RAKUTEN WAY

- Look to acquisition as a way to enter new markets.
- Look first for a cultural synergy. This will form the foundation for marketing and product development post-acquisition.

# FIVE

# REWRITING THE RULES OF CORPORATE CULTURE

## OUR FIVE PRINCIPLES

The story of the early days of Rakuten may seem very exciting, since it was a band of so few against the great big business world. But I have to confess that our small size in the early days was intentional.

When I began my business, I did so with a handful of employees. I could have had more. My job at Industrial Bank of Japan had put me in contact with many high-powered individuals in the business world, and I had forged strong relationships with them. Many had an interest in the company and were willing to support my efforts.

Still, I started small. My reason: I wanted to begin by building my corporate culture.

Corporate culture is often a feature of an organization that happens by accident. A company's traditions and expectations and processes evolve and take hold over time. Culture can come to dictate everything from behavior in the office to strategic decisions. When you ask an executive at a large company, "How did this particular tradition get started?" he may not know. He may be able to tell you only that that's the way things have always been done. That is a classic example of accidental corporate culture. No one knows why something is being done, only that it has always been that way. The longer a tradition has existed, the more entrenched it becomes.

This is a huge mistake many companies make. Culture is not something that should be left to chance or inertia. Instead, culture can be a driving force for success in a company if it is properly managed and maintained. Allowing culture to crop up in a haphazard way misses a huge opportunity. I knew this early on, and I went out of my way to make sure I did not miss it.

Many folks think that Rakuten was lucky to be so successful in such a short period of time. I respond that "luck" is really nothing more than opportunity plus preparation. Opportunities may not always be in your control, but preparation is entirely in your hands. The creation of Rakuten's corporate culture was my preparation strategy. I took the time early on to prepare the cultural foundation of the company. Then, when opportunity arose, I knew what I wanted out of it.

In this chapter, I will detail how this deliberate corporate culture created opportunity for Rakuten. I'll detail the key elements of our culture, explain why they are important, and suggest how you can incorporate them into your business. Make no mistake—a strong corporate culture is not just a "nice thing to have." It is a necessary foundation on which to build.

## THE FIVE PRINCIPLES

Walk into any room in our corporate headquarters and you'll see a poster on the wall with the Rakuten Five Principles for Success. These are the core pillars of our corporate culture, and we display them as art and have them on the back of every employee ID to continually reinforce them as our guiding themes. The five principles are:

1. Always Improve, Always Advance
2. Passionately Professional
3. Hypothesize → Practice → Validate → Shikumika (Systemize)
4. Maximize Customer Satisfaction
5. Speed!! Speed!! Speed!!

I'll discuss each in detail.

### PRINCIPLE NO. 1: ALWAYS IMPROVE, ALWAYS ADVANCE
This is the principle by which an ordinary man becomes a genius. Many make the mistake of assuming genius is a "light-bulb moment" in which some great thought or realization

magically pops into your head. And perhaps those "aha!" moments are real. But there is another way to attain genius— a way that almost anyone can pursue with enough focus and determination. That's the path of continuous improvement.

This concept of continuous improvement is one that has been made well-known by another Japanese company. As we've discussed, the auto giant Toyota made the concept world famous when it introduced the global community to its guiding principle and told everyone its Japanese name: *kaizen*. Kaizen was the watchword of the Toyota manufacturing process and it was the mandate that led the company to always focus on making better and better cars. It was kaizen that allowed Toyota to outdistance its competition and rise to a position of leadership in the global auto market.

At Rakuten, we take that manufacturing concept and apply it to people. Just as automobiles can be made better, so too can people be made better. Even more exciting, people can do this by themselves and drive their own process of kaizen.

In general, people have quite a bit of room for improvement. Most people are not working at full capacity. Most have a store of undeveloped skills. Perhaps they have never been pushed or encouraged to explore their limits. Perhaps it never even occurred to them to try. Many people are satisfied if they meet the standards set for them by their teachers, their families, or their work supervisors. Many assume that once they have graduated from school and secured a job, their efforts have paid off. But what if they undertook an attitude of kaizen? What if each individual looked within himself and made a commitment to constant improvement?

This is a concept that really excites me, because I believe there is so much untapped potential in people. Asking someone to become a genius overnight is not reasonable. But if you told that person, "Improve a little bit every day," what would those results look like over the course of a year? Ten years? An entire career? The difference is staggering.

You can look at this from a mathematical point of view. Calculate a daily increase of 1 percent for one year: 1.01 to the 365th power. The answer is 37.78. Even if you could only achieve 1 percent improvement each day—1 percent kaizen per day—at the end of one year, your result is over thirty-seven times better than when you started.

I once heard this story: A man in search of wisdom opened a book from a sword-fighting school of the Edo Period (1603–1868). Inside, there was just one phrase: "Myself of today will triumph over myself of yesterday." This is a beautifully distilled vision of kaizen. The goal is not to be great overnight, but to be better each day, knowing that this accumulation of improvements is the path to success.

Often when you look closely at a great invention or a moment of genius, you can trace the kaizen that follows in its wake. Consider Thomas Edison and the invention of the phonograph. That was a moment of great innovation, but it was also a catalyst for kaizen. Since then, innumerable engineers have followed in Edison's footsteps and given us the

Walkman, the iPod, and the state-of-the-art sound equipment we use in all forms of entertainment today. Kaizen is a process that enriches our lives in so many ways, by producing greatness over and over and over.

The beauty of kaizen as a theme of corporate culture is that anyone can pursue it. Perhaps at Toyota, on the manufacturing floor, you need specialized skills or knowledge to produce kaizen in the manufacturing process. But any individual can apply kaizen to his own work, anytime, at any level of the organization. If you apply the advice of the Edo swordsman—the "myself of today" will triumph over the "myself of yesterday"—you have the power to engineer your own kaizen.

At Rakuten, we are in a state of constant kaizen. We are already on the cutting edge of new technology, yet we are always on the hunt for new and exciting ways in which the technology is evolving. For example, we made an investment in Pinterest, a content-sharing service that allows members to "pin" images, videos, and other objects to their pinboards. Why would we do this? We already have a robust e-commerce business. The reason is that as part of our constant kaizen we are always looking for ways to improve our efforts. We are looking for new opportunities for our customers. We are looking for new ways we can improve upon the e-commerce experience. When I began to look closely at Pinterest, I could see this new evolution of e-commerce—curated commerce— as an emerging trend. This is an exciting new way that users are finding to connect using the Internet. It made perfect sense to me to find a way for Rakuten to support and participate in the next new trend in Internet activity. I'm sure Pinterest will simply be one of many avenues we pursue as we continue our efforts to always improve. There will always be a new technology, a new iteration of the way technology is used. We will be looking for those new things that represent improvement and positive change.

Sometimes improvements can be painful. When we started Rakuten, we opened for business with a structure that allowed for merchants to pay only a fixed monthly fee. When we grew to a certain size, it became clear that we could no longer afford to maintain that pay structure. We improved the system by adding to the fixed monthly fee a percentage of each merchant's profits.

This was not an easy change to make. Naturally, the merchants objected. But we could not keep the original system just because "that's the way it's always been done." The Rakuten way is not to hold on to a process for the sake of history. The Rakuten way is to always improve. The change was necessary, and we did our best to communicate that to our merchants. We explained how it would improve the fortunes of everyone in the Rakuten ecosystem—merchant, customer, and headquarters.

We see evidence of kaizen in the marketplace around us. When you look at the differences between the corporate cultures at Google and many software companies, the kaizen principle comes to light. Google is famous for coming up with ideas and, if they don't take off, ditching them and moving on. Many software companies, on the other hand, are constantly at work on their products, with new versions emerging on the marketplace as improvements are made. This is a kaizen culture. Just because the product launched does not mean the team can move on and forget about it. In fact, just the opposite is true. That product is under constant review. The team is always looking for improvements—even that 1 percent improvement—that will inch everyone forward toward genius.

Think of yourself as a software program or an automobile engine. Are you working at full capacity? Could you improve? What can you do today—what can you do every day—to be better? Don't wait for the "big leap" forward. Instead, focus on daily improvements. Some will be big and some will be small. But if constant, they will add up to a giant step forward.

Advice to readers: adopting kaizen begins with a good eye for the absurd. Which rules and traditions are acting as obstacles? What are the processes that everyone does without thinking? Those are your first targets for improvement. Refuse to tolerate old, absurd rules in silence. Challenge and revise them in the spirit of kaizen.

## PRINCIPLE NO. 2: PASSIONATELY PROFESSIONAL

What does it mean to be a professional? I believe I use the word somewhat differently than most people do. For many, the word "professional" just means a skilled individual—someone trained to carry out certain tasks that an amateur couldn't.

I take it a step further in my own life. To me, a professional is someone who takes his work to heart and makes it not just a source of income, but a source of pride and joy. That's why, when I created the second of our Rakuten principles, I didn't say just: be professional. I said: be passionately professional. That emotional undercurrent is the critical component.

There are many successful professionals in the world. But only the passionate professionals are capable of greatness. Most "professionals" are just going through the motions, completing their assigned tasks, staying out of trouble, and inching up the corporate ladder. Those individuals are earning a living, but they are not advancing themselves, their company, or the human race in any significant way. When one is passionately professional, on the other hand, one is driven to do that work—whatever it is—at the highest possible level for the greatest possible good. That adds joy to the experience, whatever your profession may be.

I have a favorite old movie starring Hitoshi Ueki and the members of the Japanese comedy/jazz band the Crazy Cats. The movie depicts a stereotypical Japanese office, in which workers come in every day and, ignoring the stacks of paper around them, do nothing but play cards and wait for retirement. In the movie, the protagonist makes the outrageous move of diving in and processing all the papers and documents that have piled up around the office. No matter how many times I watch this movie, I always laugh at the scene in which the character moves like a gleeful tornado around the office, plowing through the piles of paperwork, making order and forward progress out of the neglected stacks. His energy and emotion are contagious. It makes me want to leave for work that very moment and do the same.

This is the mind-set of the passionate professional. This is the energy and the drive and the passion with which I ask everyone at Rakuten to approach our daily lives. It is, as the movie shows, merely a question of mental positioning. Those stacks of papers were not interesting or challenging to the movie's hero—until he forced himself to look at them in that way. You must look at your tasks as a challenge in order to find the joy in daily work. Anything can be interesting in the right mental framework. If I told you to drive one hundred times around the loop that surrounds Tokyo, you might think that sounds tedious. But if I told you it was a race, you would find those same one hundred laps far more engaging.

This mental challenge can be present in any part of a workday. Even when faced with a rudimentary task such as storing inventory, you can find a way to be passionately professional in your efforts. You could find ways to do the task more efficiently, using fewer materials, or finishing more quickly. You could find ways to do the job that would affect those around you in a positive way. You could look for ways to apply what you have learned in this task to other tasks that would improve your productivity. Every task merits a passionately professional effort.

If your job involves processing paperwork, this too can be an area in which you can inject challenge and joy. When I was at a Japanese bank, I was initially assigned to the foreign currency division, where paperwork was the norm. I was always challenging myself to find ways to improve efficiency and eliminate mistakes. I was constantly thinking, *How can I improve this process? What can I do to be more effective and improve the lives of those around me?* It may seem like a platitude, but when you feel your job is truly benefiting someone else, even the most seemingly insignificant task can be fun.

Thanks to my time processing all that paperwork, I came to understand the role of paperwork in a larger operation. Years later, when I opened my own company, that insight was a powerful weapon for me. I'm certain that if I'd just done my job at IBJ with a sense of boredom and obligation, I never would have learned anything valuable in that period of my working life. Because I strove to be passionately professional about my paperwork, I was able to both contribute to the company and take away valuable insights that served me well later in my life. If I had not taken that passionately professional approach to my work at IBJ, perhaps Rakuten would not exist today.

There are no inherently interesting jobs, just people who make a job interesting with their passionately professional approach. The person who finds joy and challenge cleaning the corridor or processing the paperwork is a passionate professional. That individual will go far.

Advice to readers: consider the fishmonger. There is a great story in the Rakuten files of a fishmonger who was interviewed by a city journalist about his job. "There is nothing as interesting as fish," he told the journalist. "I just don't get why everyone in the world doesn't want to be a fisherman. This has always been a mystery to me." No matter what you do, if you do it well and with passion, you will achieve success and happiness.

## PRINCIPLE NO. 3: HYPOTHESIZE → PRACTICE → VALIDATE → *SHIKUMIKA*

Careful readers of my writings on culture will notice that the word "shikumika" is relatively new to my construct of this third principle. In fact, the full principle reads: Hypothesize → Practice → Validate → Shikumika. ("Shikumika" is the Japanese word for "systemize.") While each part is important, the final word was the last to join the string.

In this principle, I ask Rakuten employees to ensure that the best ideas rise to the top. When you look at the first two principles—kaizen and passionately professional—you can see two ways that I have encouraged employees to strive for greatness and go above and beyond the parameters of their daily assignments. Given those instructions, it's important to have a clear framework for all that passion and improvement so that it does not create chaos. This framework comes from the concept and practice of shikumika.

The process of achieving shikumika is not as complex as it sounds. In fact, we have all been doing it for most of our lives. Think, for example, of children playing in a sandbox. One child makes a mountain with sand. Another brings water from the drinking fountain and pours it over the mountain, making a river. This is fun, so everyone tries it. Soon everyone is bored. Then one child says, "What if we used a bucket to carry the water?" They try that but the sand mountain collapses. Now the children say, "What if we built a bigger sand mountain?"

That looks like play, but in fact it is the very process I am advocating in this section. Those children in the sandbox are acting out the principle of Hypothesize → Practice → Validate → Shikumika. They are putting out ideas, trying them out, considering the results, deciding whether they have reached the right process or if they need to go back and try some more. This is a consummately human process. Early humans used it to try out different tools. We use it today on the sports field and, of course, in science.

This process is often lacking in the business world, which is why I highlight it as a key principle of our corporate culture. When you enter the business world, you often get an implicit directive to stop experimenting and start following orders. Few managers advise new recruits to think on their own. They want their employees to do as they're told. The problem with that is that new recruits simply learn the art of following orders and they lose the skills of the sandbox—the skills that let them think and try and experiment. Over time, those skills fade completely, and you are left with a company full of people who can follow orders but can't do much else.

If we are to be a company that constantly improves, we must have a spirit of experimentation. In order to do that without chaos, we must give Rakuten employees the system in which to experiment usefully.

A hypothesis begins with a game of catch between the left brain and the right brain. A spark of inspiration ignites the right brain, and it pairs with the logic of the left brain to become a scientific hypothesis. People tend to emphasize the right brain when talking about inspiration and new ideas. But the left brain is equally critical. Inspiration is not always usable. The left brain gives us a framework to help us evaluate our right-brain inspirations—are they realistic? Will they confer advantage? The left brain enables this next step.

So start with a hypothesis, apply the left-brain framework and try it out, then look at your results and see if they validate your hypothesis. If you get a positive result, move to the final step in our chain: shikumika (systemize). Take your idea and make it into a process that can be followed. I added shikumika to this chain of events as I realized over time that a great idea is useful only when one then puts it into practice.

Here's an example of this cultural principle at work at Rakuten. In an effort to improve our retention of interested customers, we tested a theory in our headquarters. We instituted a rule that every sales inquiry made on our website would be responded to immediately via a phone call by one of our representatives. We termed this the "two-minute call." Every new customer would receive a phone call within two minutes.

Would this be useful to us? Would it help us cement our connection with customers? It did. In our test, we found customers astounded and pleased that they heard from Rakuten so quickly. They responded positively to the message we were sending—we are vitally interested in you, so much so that we will respond to your web contact with all due speed.

It was then ready to be systemized for use more widely in Rakuten. But it required systematic testing before we were willing to tinker with our original process.

Sometimes the hypothesis does not pan out. After having the idea, testing it, and practicing it, word comes back: no, that doesn't work. When that happens, we have not failed. We can be secure in our knowledge that we fully explored the possibility. Ideas that are never tested linger like smoke in the air and distract everyone with what might have been. When you follow through with a standard process of exploration and testing, even an unsuccessful idea helps the company move forward. Once tested, the idea can be put to rest and everyone can move his or her energies on to the next challenge.

While we practice shikumika in our business process, we also carry it out scientifically in our research labs, the Rakuten Institute of Technology. Within the R&D framework, we apply the same process to new concepts in technology. Just as it helps us in business, this rigorous process of innovation and experimentation indicates which new technological processes we should systemize next.

Advice to readers: in setting up a structured framework to encourage exploration of new ideas, you must also be willing to see some of these ideas fail. The only way workers will fully pursue experiments is if they feel assured that they will not be punished for an unsuccessful outcome. To find great ideas that should be systemized, you must accept all outcomes of the experimenting process.

## PRINCIPLE NO. 4: MAXIMIZE CUSTOMER SATISFACTION

Like kaizen, this is a concept that is already quite well-known around the world. But again, I have my own spin on this popular idea. There are many companies that devote themselves to customer satisfaction, but they focus only on their one, final customer—the end user of the product. In my mind, this is not the only customer who can be satisfied. A business is connected to many groups of people. The end users are an important group, to be sure. But they are not the only customers.

When I talk about maximizing customer satisfaction, I am not thinking about only the end user—for instance, the woman who will buy rice from a Rakuten merchant. I look instead at all the "customers" who exist in my ecosystem. That rice merchant is also my customer. Should I not also want to maximize his satisfaction?

This is a somewhat radical idea. Most companies—even those who consider themselves stars in customer satisfaction—are not focused on the vendors or merchants in this process. When Zappos sells shoes, the company focuses on "delivering happiness" to the end user—that is, the customer who buys the shoes. While Zappos makes an effort to create good vendor relationships, its focus is ultimately on getting a "wow" from the final customer.

The same is true at Amazon. Amazon is devoted to providing the most efficient experience for the customer—that is, the individual shopper clicking away at his computer. But I would bet Amazon does not spend as much time or effort on the vendor who supplies the product that end consumer will eventually own. To Amazon—indeed, to most companies that tout their customer-satisfaction process today—it's the end user who is important, and no one else.

I don't subscribe to this definition of customer satisfaction. In my mind, the customer is important, but not god. The satisfaction of the merchant is also part of my job. When I look to maximize customer satisfaction, I want that effort to reach all my customers—my vendors and merchants and end users. They are all part of my satisfaction profile. No group should be sacrificed for another's happiness.

Consider, for example, the story of one of our merchants, Koh Takagi, who runs a successful fashion company via the Rakuten platform. His operation was a quick success with customers—his revenues shot from zero to a monthly gross of thirty million yen (over $340,000) in just four months. Clearly, his end customers were very, very happy. They were handing over more and more money to his company. But as that success emerged, life for Takagi and his employees became intense and stressful. "We started living in the office," he recalls. "It was a struggle just to ensure all items were dispatched."

What got him through his early, frenzied days? Daily telephone calls and meetings with his Rakuten consultant. We were able to provide this entrepreneur with help regarding sales, web-page design, even a bigger warehouse. We helped him make his customers happy by helping him remain happy in his work.

It's my opinion that this creates greater satisfaction for all. Our competitor's customers may be happy to be getting their books quickly and cheaply, but they are not blind and deaf to the unhappiness generated in the vendor and merchant community by some policies. Major marketplace vendors have complained about their inability to market to customers acquired from purchases on the marketplace. They resent the marketplace acting as both a host and competitor, with the power to underprice them. This undermines the loyalty of a marketplace customer. It opens them to the offering of a competing company—especially one that is more respectful of the vendor community and uses that as part of its value proposition.

Another note regarding customer satisfaction: I understand that this imperative does not apply just to the Rakuten employees who work directly with our merchants. Customer satisfaction must apply to all of us, even to me. What am I, as the CEO, doing every day to maximize customer satisfaction?

One way I pursue this goal is through my personal use of social media. I am a frequent user of social media to promote my own business and my larger ideas for business in Japan and the world. I used Twitter to get my ideas out into the conversation. My tweets spanned a range of topics. Often I posted interesting articles I come across that relate to business or economic news in Japan or the global marketplace. Many times I used Twitter to talk about important developments inside Rakuten. And once in a while, I simply commented on a great ramen restaurant. I have moved on to embrace new social media platforms, but my interest in the tactic remains high. All my social media postings have a purpose: they are designed to keep me in the conversation and to make it clear that I consider this channel a vital business conversation—not just an platform for idle chitchat.

Not all CEOs are involved in social media, and this may be a mistake. It's not uncommon for those who have reached the highest levels of a company to consider social media a lesser tool—something for the young people to play with. They may support it as a tool for their marketing departments to deploy, but they don't embrace it as a tool for their own leadership efforts. This is a missed opportunity. Social media tools can be a powerful tool for thought leadership. When you want to communicate your strategic thinking on a broad scale along with your insights into global happenings, social media allow you to do this in real time, without the lag of a traditional publication or speech. Instead of reacting to events, you are part of them as they unfold in the marketplace.

What's more, the relationship between CEO and customer has changed in recent years. Today, customers are not satisfied with a faceless leader. They want to know the individual who runs the company. They are interested in personalities. When we take the role of leadership in a company, we must embrace this reality.

Even when I used Twitter, I kept my mind open to the new tools that might come along. I see social media as more than just a tool to increase sales or even a tool to manage my business. It is also a tool I can leverage in my role as a leader in the wider business community. All leaders should look for ways to better communicate their vision and their insights. Social media present that opportunity. And they present me with a way to deliver the kind of relationship customers have come to expect in the always-on marketplace.

## PRINCIPLE NO. 5: SPEED!! SPEED!! SPEED!!

I cannot overemphasize the importance of this last principle. Later in this book, we will devote an entire chapter to the practice of speed at Rakuten—that's how important it is to us and, I believe, to the success of business in general today.

Here's how it functions as a pillar of our culture.

One great thing about a very new, very small business is that things happen quickly. Someone has a great idea; it is tested and vetted immediately. Someone gets a great tip on a new business option, and the company can swiftly move to take advantage. This speed is a wonderful strength of a small, entrepreneurial company. I found it inspiring and effective when Rakuten was small. So I looked for a way to keep it part of the company, even as we grew large.

The answer, I've discovered, is to not accept the expected slowness of a large organization but instead to continue demanding speed as the organization grows. This is not always easy. But I believe it is vital to any company's success.

I am always looking for ways to help Rakuten move faster. For example, as the company grew, I grew frustrated with the length of meetings. To shorten them, I suggested a rule in which everyone would distribute an agenda the day before the meeting. This allowed everyone to come to meetings prepared and not waste time explaining to everyone why we were all there.

That is a fairly straightforward example. Another practice I have adopted revolves around the use of social media. I have always placed great emphasis on communication in this company. I have set in place many formal measures to be sure there is communication and transparency at all times in this firm. I encourage my employees to discuss and share information, insights, even problems they may be encountering. The more we communicate, the more we can help one another achieve the broader company goals. I hold weekly company-wide meetings. I have even made a common language a priority for everyone in the company from myself down to the newest recruit.

But formal communication is only one part of my strategy. I also want Rakuten team members to communicate informally—in part, because it is often faster than the formal route. And for that, I turn to social media.

Rakuten is a big user of Yammer, an internal social network designed specifically for enterprise use. Yammer is like an open conversation going on in the company all the time. It is a virtual gathering place for conversations. Individuals can post questions, comments, ideas, and reports.

As part of my strategy, I have been encouraging Rakuten employees to use Yammer as a way to share their ideas and keep the cross conversations flowing. When a company grows large and is spread out among many countries as we are today, communications can often break down. Time zones can make phone calls and video conferences tricky. Cost and time can make physical travel a burden. This makes a social network even more critical. To make sure we are all sharing our information, a social network is necessary to support the conversation. On Yammer, you may find the text of recent speeches I have given. You will see individuals who participated in training programs reporting back on what they have learned. You will see technologists in one location posting a question and others elsewhere posting answers.

This is the cross conversation of a company at work. If we all worked in one building, this is the kind of chatter that would take place naturally in the hallways, in the cafeteria, in the elevator. But as we grow, technology allows us to continue these conversations uninterrupted by time and distance. Without these cross conversations, we would become isolated from one another. Great ideas may go unnoticed, problems may take longer to solve, and leadership opportunities may be lost. Just as I encourage Rakuten merchants to use social media to stay in touch, I insist that Rakuten employees do the same within the company. In a fast-moving world, there is often no time to wait for a face-to-face meeting or even a phone call to resolve an issue or discuss a problem. Social media offer us the chance to handle these communications in real time—and companies that communicate in this virtual world have an edge over those that are sitting on the social media sidelines.

As a company grows, there are many roadblocks to speed. Often, workers value caution, and that works against speed. Everyone wants to hang back and see how the leadership will go, allowing them to follow rather than lead. To counter this, I've made it clear that I desire speed, not perfection. I would rather make quick forward progress and then fix what is wrong along the way than hold back until all possible fixes have been made. Waiting for perfection is not an option. Without speed, a company cannot lead.

## THE FUTURE OF OUR CULTURE

As we grow and expand, my primary goal is to keep our culture intact. When we look for acquisitions in the global marketplace, we consider whether that company will be a good fit with our culture. When we buy a company or enter a new market, we send out an "ambassador" to help the newcomers acclimate to the Rakuten Way.

For all our devotion to technology, there are some things new technology cannot replace.

First, the Asakai. Every Tuesday morning, everyone in my company gathers for a company-wide meeting. Everyone. Two thousand people make their way to the meeting space in Rakuten headquarters. Video hookups are arranged so that divisions around the globe can dial in and participate. It is a full company gathering and it happens every week. It is mandatory that everyone in the company attend.

After all my praise of social media, why do I still insist on this weekly meeting? Because social media can't replace the emphasis of a company-wide gathering. As much as we can learn and understand from social media, it is still just text coming to us on a screen. The power of a live meeting, with reports made by executives around the globe, still carries more weight. You may be able to ignore or give just a small amount of attention to a posting on a social network site. But you can't miss the weekly meeting, and when you are in the meeting, you can't help but pay attention to the speakers. So far, nothing I have seen in technology can compare to the impact of my addressing the entire company live every week.

The second element that can't be replaced is travel. Social media can make communication across time and space easier, but I have not yet seen it become a replacement for live meetings. I still travel all the time. I travel to the annual meetings of Rakuten merchants to meet with them and hear their experiences. I suppose social media could be leveraged so that this annual meeting could be held virtually, but I fear it would never be able to capture the passion and power of the live meeting. Human beings gather in part because they derive energy from one another. While social media might be able to make a conversation connection, it cannot replace the energy that surges in a room when a big group has come together to share success stories.

Travel is also critically important to me as Rakuten grows and we make more acquisitions around the world. Certainly, social media will allow us to converse routinely with our new partners in Europe and Asia and North and South America. But face-to-face visits, in which we all meet and get to know one another, are still critical to the process of learning to function as a whole.

Finally, common language. I have already discussed in depth my reasoning for making English the common language of Rakuten and for making the Englishnization of the company a top priority. I revisit that topic here to say that social media can't replace real conversation—and to be effective real conversation must take place without the lag time of an interpreter. Even as my team becomes skilled in using social media to communicate, I have not let up on my goal of getting everyone at Rakuten to a skilled level of English-language conversation.

Our culture built our company. Although I use technology to advance it, ultimately our culture is a system of shared beliefs and goals. It represents the core themes we pursue, no matter where we are in the world, no matter what project we undertake on any given day. I believe that will remain true as long as we're in business.

## TRY THE RAKUTEN WAY

- Start your company with the creation of a culture.
- Put your cultural rules in writing.
- Make culture a part of the day-to-day operations of your company.

# SIX

# REWRITING THE RULES OF THE INTERNET

## A TOOL FOR EMPOWERMENT, SPEED, AND JOY

You may think you know the Internet, but you don't.

Web technology has become ingrained in so many aspects of our lives that it feels like second nature. Many savvy entrepreneurs have leveraged the Internet to create powerful and far-reaching businesses. These businesses reach into our everyday lives so effortlessly that we forget the Internet has much more to offer. Conventional wisdom assumes that the Internet is a tool with a defined set of functions. In fact, if you believe many of the current leaders in e-commerce, it's a tool for efficiency, profit, and standardization.

It can be all those things. But it is not limited to those things. In this chapter, I will discuss my execution of e-commerce and how it differs from the positions others have taken in the space. I will lay out my vision for the Internet and explain why it is not just a vision for my company, but also a vision for the world and for humanity.

The Internet is not limited to the vision put forth by some successful companies today. There is another way. The Rakuten Way. This chapter will reveal our unique vision for this world-changing technology.

## WHAT IS THE INTERNET?

The Internet is not a vending machine. If I could leave you with one piece of information after reading this book, it would be that. Many of the leaders in the e-commerce industry have leveraged the Internet to create a kind of global vending machine in which consumers punch in their orders and their credit card numbers and the machine spits out a product. Some of our competitors have made quite a bit of money with this vending machine method—so much so that most people assume this is the best way to use the Internet in global commerce.

I'd argue that this is a shortsighted and limited view of the Internet. The vending machine process can take us only so far. It can deliver some goods with efficiency and speed, but it cannot embrace all that the endless global array of vendors has to offer. And it can't deliver the maximum satisfaction the customer wants and deserves. The vending machine philosophy is a reasonable start. But the Internet could be so much more to both customers and vendors. Here's how.

## THE INTERNET IS A TOOL FOR COLLABORATION

The Internet is a huge new opportunity for like-minded people to meet and exchange information. Collaboration is possible in a way that it never was before.

The technology allows for a give-and-take of information that supports a new level of collaboration among a variety of players—for example, between vendor and merchant. In the pre-Internet days, retail moved in a linear fashion—an assembly line of supply. The vendor would create goods and deliver them to the merchant. The merchant would sell them to the consumer. Each player knew his place on the assembly line and there was no need—indeed, there was no way—for the players to circumvent the system. Merchandise moved in a straight line from the manufacturer to the end user.

The Internet takes that straight line and refashions it into a continuous loop. When the players in the retail process are able to collaborate, they can support one another, provide one another with valuable information, and create a situation in which all parties are better-off. This is especially true for Rakuten's online mall and its individual merchants. The individual merchants create goods and services and the Rakuten mall delivers them to the end user—the customer. But this is not a linear relationship. Rakuten leverages Internet technology so that each player in the process has contact with the others. The merchant can market directly to the customer. The customer can email the merchant with questions or comments. Rakuten can offer advice and support to the merchant.

The customer can use Rakuten to find out about other products he might want to buy.

While the original retail process moved in a straight line, this new retail experience, enabled by the Internet, is a circular ecosystem. All the parties can communicate, share information, ask questions, and benefit from the experience. The merchant sells more of his products; the customer has a richer, more satisfying experience; and Rakuten reaps a profit from both relationships. The collaboration makes all parties happier than they were in the linear retail experience.

We envisioned this collaborative process from the very beginning. When we began our mall, we recruited our first merchants with the promise of collaboration—and we backed it up from the start. We did more than just offer the merchants a chance to participate in our technology; we joined hands and made that technological leap with them.

We also opened the lines of communication to encourage collaboration not just with us, but also with customers. We decided early on that email communication would be open— that the merchants and customers could deal with one another directly. As we have discussed previously, this is not how most Internet malls were designed at the time. Many acted as gatekeepers and facilitated the email conversation between vendor and merchant. We took away this barrier and allowed another level of collaboration between merchant and customer. The results were remarkable.

One of our earliest merchants was a jewelry designer named Chie Naito. She created a unique jewelry line that blended Japanese craftsmanship with sophisticated European designs. She traveled frequently to Europe to take photographs and be inspired for new creations. Her work was consistently beautiful and well crafted. But what made her an Internet success story was her ability to communicate with her customers.

Via her Rakuten e-commerce platform, Naito built a dedicated community of fans. She posted her thoughts about her work and photographs of her travels. Her customers responded, posting their own comments and engaging in online conversation with one another. Customers grew so tight as a community that they fashioned a nickname for themselves—Beneller—a takeoff on the store's name, Bene Bene.

Naito says that when she meets a regular customer for the first time at an offline event, it is "like greeting an old friend."

"People said it is impossible to build deep relationships with customers over the Internet, but we did it," she says.

Our more recent merchants met with similar experiences. One seller of DJ equipment opened his Tokyo shop at the same time he joined the Rakuten e-commerce community. Taisuke Ichihara's goal was to provide the same level of service both on- and offline. The key to doing that, he says, is the ability to communicate with customers. He maintains a Rakuten blog with more than five thousand subscribers. And it's not unusual for one of his blog fans to pop into the store for a visit. "Readers from as far afield as Korea and China have turned up," he says. The virtual conversation allows Ichihara to take his retail offering to a new level. "We aren't just selling

DJ kits here. We are building a community where people can enjoy music."

There are many more stories like these. Opening the communication channel has been a boon to all manner of retailers in our Rakuten ecosystem. Customers were able to say what they liked and didn't like about products. Merchants were able to get that crucial information firsthand and incorporate it into their future business efforts. We at Rakuten continued to benefit from the greater satisfaction of both vendor and merchant. Opening up the email channel was just another way we encouraged collaboration—and the Internet was the tool that made that collaboration possible.

Collaboration is not just a retail tool. We reap its many benefits in many other ways. The Internet allows our company to function on the global stage—our employees can collaborate across timelines and oceans seamlessly and swiftly. We are able to share information, ideas, and experiences in a way that pre-Internet companies could only dream of. This not only makes global expansion possible, it also makes it consistently profitable.

Our emphasis on collaboration is not just a way to differentiate our business. In my opinion, it is the only way to achieve sustained success. If you use the Internet to control commerce—as early Internet malls did, and as some Internet companies continue to do today—you risk having your success run out. Eventually, the parties involved will tire of the control you exert and will look for other options, if they exist. They will leave for more freedom, more possibilities.

Human beings naturally want to be the masters of their fate. So I follow my process of collaboration not just because it is profitable, but also because it fits more organically with the way human beings want to live in the world.

## THE INTERNET IS A TOOL FOR JOY

While many have focused on the way the Internet can make money, I like to remember that the Internet can be a force for happiness. This brings me quite naturally to my next topic: how the Internet is a tool for joy.

This may seem like an intellectual detour for an e-commerce company, but it's actually a very important part of my philosophy. The Internet, as wielded by some other leaders in e-commerce, has taken on a very strict, stern image. For example, if you do business with other marketplaces, you will find that the templates are set and the processes are rigidly controlled. The look of the pages is consistent and there is little room for expression or deviance.

This is how our competitors do it. Efficiency and control all the way.

How much fun is that? Not much. I would argue that if you take all the fun out of the Internet experience, you negate a primary purpose of this technology in the world today. Customers don't come to the Internet just for efficiency. They come to have fun.

If you look at what has happened to online shopping, you can see the desire for fun and entertainment. Customers don't visit only the online brands they've already heard of. They love to discover something new and interesting. They want to share this information with their friends via social networks. They talk online about their experiences with the store and the product. Online shopping is not simply a utilitarian experience. It is entertainment.

This is really not surprising when we look at how consumers have always approached shopping—as part chore, part entertainment. In the old days, going to the market was a chance to do business and to socialize with neighbors. In more recent years, shopping malls were built to sell goods and provide a new kind of marketplace for shoppers to gather. Malls became palaces of entertainment, complete with food and roller coasters and other diversions to enjoy while shopping. It is no surprise that the consumer carries this desire to combine fun and shopping to the online experience. For this reason, we are always looking for ways to make the Rakuten shopping experience entertaining. We were inspired by the early marketplaces such as the Rakuichi Rakuza—the first free-trade market in Japan launched by a famous samurai general. We understand, too, that the modern consumer has come online to buy a product. But the consumer is also looking for entertainment. We create our online experience so that it delivers fun and enjoyment as well as a product.

One way this happens is in our page design. Our competitors look for ways to make their pages more efficient, so that the customer can click on a product more quickly, get to the register more quickly, pay, and leave in a hurry. Where is the entertainment in that experience? Our pages assume the customer wants what she has always wanted from retail: an entertaining shopping experience. Our pages employ a technology that allows for a constant scroll—no need to click away and be done. Stay on the page and explore; perhaps you will experience the joy of discovering something new, something surprising, just as you might have done in the brick-and-mortar world. The shopping experience should not be reduced to a few dull clicks. The Internet can deliver the joy of real shopping—why should the consumer settle for the less entertaining alternative?

Much of what is going on in e-commerce today misses the joy and entertainment of online shopping. After the dot-com bust, many focused their attention so tightly on profits that they made Internet shopping into an efficiency machine. This ignores the reason human beings shop as much as they do. Clearly, we shop for more than just necessities. We shop to discover new things. We shop to enjoy the experience of discovery. The marketplace—whether real or virtual—is a gathering place.

Reminding everyone to notice the joy in the Internet is not always easy. Over the years, plenty of negative emotions have been associated with the Internet and with technology in general. I remember back in the late 1990s as the turn of the century approached. It seemed like everyone was in a panic over "Y2K." This was true in Japan and indeed all over the developed world. The fear was that a programming glitch would kick in as the clocks turned over from 1999 to 2000 and computers would fail all over the world. Bank

ATMs would freeze. Airplanes would lose their navigation. Elevators would stop mid-rise. Some were so worried that they stocked up on supplies as the New Year approached. The mood around technology was decidedly apprehensive. The change in calendar was making us all wonder: Would our technology turn out to have been a bad idea?

Of course now we all know the answer to that. The year 2000 dawned and nothing bad happened. Our computers continued to function. Our planes did not fall from the sky. The technology we had come to rely on was still reliable. But the event revealed an underlying trepidation about technology and its role in our lives. It revealed that many people all over the world were not convinced that technology was always a good thing. In fact, they wondered if it was something we should fear.

I did not pay much attention to the Y2K panic when it was happening. I was too busy recruiting new retailers for my online shopping mall. There was no doubt in my mind that technology—and the Internet specifically—was a positive development.

This potential for joy is one of the reasons I got into the Internet business in the first place. After I left IBJ, I spent some time trying to decide what new company I would start. I closely examined several interesting businesses. I looked into starting a microbrewery. I investigated a line of bakeries. These businesses had potential. I could have made money in either of them. But it was the Internet that excited me. There was so much possibility there, and I knew I would never be bored. It was a business that would always keep me challenged and that would be a perennial source of joy for me.

I did not leave IBJ to get into the business of vending machines. The "e" in e-commerce can also stand for entertainment. There is no reason for the fear of new technology to take over, as it did during the Y2K period. E-commerce can and does provide an example of how technology enriches our lives and creates opportunity, possibility, and connection on a global scale. It is a theme we embrace at Rakuten in every aspect of our business. There is no reason to leave joy behind.

## THE INTERNET IS A TOOL FOR SPEED

Perhaps the most obvious benefit the Internet brings to the planet is its ability to hasten communications. When information travels at the speed of a click, all manner of activities speed up along with it.

Rakuten was still a two-man operation when I had my moment of realization about the Internet and speed. I came into the office one day and my one colleague was reading the *Wall Street Journal* on his computer screen. This was back in the late 1990s, when all things Internet were still quite new and evolving. I looked closely at my colleague's screen and realized he was reading the same day's issue. This was a huge moment for me.

Before the Internet, reading the *Wall Street Journal* in Japan required quite a bit of time and effort. Copies of the newspaper had to be printed in the United States, then placed on an airplane to Tokyo and picked up at the airport before a consumer in Japan could buy and read them. Often, as a Japanese consumer, I was reading a *Wall Street Journal* that was at least a day (sometimes two days) old. It was the best I could do, so I put up with it. But the day I saw my colleague reading the *Wall Street Journal* in real time online, I knew the Internet had wrought a major change in business. It was taking time out of the business process. Whatever else the technology would offer us one day, at the moment the benefit was clear: speed.

Internet speed does more than just get products to market more quickly. It can also take time out of the entire business cycle—everything can happen more quickly. Consider the route a Japanese product or custom takes to get to the American market. When I was a boy and lived with my family in Connecticut for two years, it was widely believed that Americans would never really take to sushi. It was too unfamiliar to their Western palates. That changed, of course. Today there are sushi restaurants all over the United States. But it took years for that to happen. Now look at another food item that got its start in Japan—bubble tea. That began as a fad in Japan and took off in the United States within months. Why? News spreads more quickly now. When there is a new product in one country, customers in another can easily find out about it. They can hear from other consumers why it is desirable. This communication speeds the product cycle. While it took years of travel and experience to bring sushi to the United States, it took just a few weeks and a few clicks for bubble tea to make the same journey. The Internet is the most invaluable tool we have for speed in all industries.

## THE INTERNET IS A TOOL FOR IMPROVING THE HUMAN CONDITION

I differ from my e-commerce competitors in many ways, but nowhere is this more obvious than in my social mission. For me, the Internet and the business of e-commerce are more than just a way to make a living. As I stated earlier, I had other options when I started my business. My possibilities were not limited. I chose the Internet in part because I could see that in addition to building a company, I could improve the lives of others around me.

No company can be truly great unless it is doing something to make life on this planet better. And there are so many ways an Internet company can improve life.

The Internet, as I see it, provides a platform for small and midsize businesses to thrive. Before the Internet became a force in business, we were hurtling toward a place in commerce where the small and midsize companies were endangered. Many of the retail districts that once held thriving mom-and-pop businesses had lost their traffic to large corporate shopping malls. And retail wasn't the only sector undergoing a consolidation. Many other industries were also contracting. The smaller firms were being squeezed out.

The advent of the Internet as a business platform gave new life and new prospects to the small-business owner. For me, this was a very exciting reason to get into an Internet-related business. It was more than just a way for me to make money; it was a way for an entire segment of the population to make money. This put my efforts as a businessman into a new category. It raised the purpose of my company from making money to improving the human condition.

I keep a book in my office. It is a collection of stories from the Rakuten files. Each chapter is a profile of a Rakuten merchant. There are many emotional stories in this collection. One is the story of a family fabric business. It was founded in 1928. For years, the family patriarch washed cotton in the river that ran past the building and laid it out to dry on the banks. It was a small, specialized business. But by the time the grandson took over the firm, the company was in trouble. Cheap fabric imports from China had come into the market-place and the tiny fabric maker could not compete on price. Wholesalers would no longer do business with him.

The grandson, who had only recently stepped into his position as the company's chief executive, made a decision to shift the company's sales channel. It continued to pursue its traditional cloth-dyeing and bleaching techniques—but instead of dealing with wholesalers, the grandson opened a Rakuten shop and began to target a new market: moms. He reached out to his end users directly—filling the store's virtual newsletter with information about what made his fabric special. He wrote about the techniques he used to ensure that the fabric was of high quality. He wrote about the people who made the fabric and their dedication to quality and safety standards. He was able to shift the positioning of this product from price to quality. In this way, he kept his doors open and his staff employed.

Another story from the book goes back even further into Japan's history. Taketora is a company in a remote region of Japan engaged in the art of making items from a unique strain of bamboo—a variety that grows only in the hills around its company headquarters. Fourth-generation CEO Yoshihiro Yamagishi says the Internet saved his family's business. "If we hadn't started selling online, the business probably wouldn't have survived." That would have been more than an economic tragedy, he says. It would have meant the loss of the specialized art his family had helped create. "Bamboo has special power," he says. "If you put just one thing made of bamboo on your table at home, you'll notice. It is part of the Japanese soul."

These are the stories that tell me I was right to make my business an Internet company rather than a brewery or a bakery chain. The Internet can change people's lives in ways that were not possible before the technology came into wide usage.

No company can be truly great if it is out only to be financially successful. A business that improves the human condition is one that will truly thrive. The Internet is the tool that allows me to do that with my business.

And of course this technology has an impact far beyond the business world. The Internet allows human beings to make faster and more meaningful connections than ever before. It allows people raised within the confines of one national culture or language to reach across borders and gain understanding. It is my dream that the Internet will facilitate not only commerce across borders, but also greater human empathy and cooperation across borders. Someday, traditional borders based on language and culture and national identity may even fade, as the Internet encourages humanity to function as one connected people.

As I build and expand my business, I consider it a stepping-stone toward that new world. Perhaps people of different cultures first become acquainted by engaging in e-commerce. Where might that initial connection lead? If you can connect across borders to do business, what other problems can you connect to solve? The Internet makes virtually any scale of change possible. Throughout human history, many great connections between disparate cultures were forged first by trade. Doing business together naturally leads to learning about one another and finding commonalities.

This vision of a borderless world is a driving force in my Internet philosophy. As my competitors look for ways to use the Internet to rein in commerce—to make it more efficient, faster, more controlled—I look for ways that the Internet can fuel change. I provide an Internet ecosystem that encourages creative experimentation. I don't know exactly what my efforts will inspire in others. But I know we will need these great new ideas for our businesses to grow, our cultures to thrive, and our life on this planet to be the best it can be.

I know one thing: great ideas don't come from a vending machine.

## THE NEW VIRTUAL FRONTIER: SOCIAL MEDIA

Even as we have grown as an e-commerce company and thrived using tools such as blogs and email, new tools and new platforms have continued to proliferate. We are always on the hunt for the next platform. Although it is still relatively new, we are deeply involved in social media.

In 2011, I resigned from a high-profile business group called Keidanren. I differed with the leadership over its position regarding energy policy in Japan. It was a rather ordinary business dispute except for one thing: I opted to resign in an extraordinary way. I made my announcement via Twitter. This was notable for many reasons. Keidanren is an old and, in many ways, an old-fashioned organization. Something as serious as a resignation was not traditionally carried out in a public venue. In the old days, my break with the group would have been carried out behind closed doors, with an exchange of private paperwork. My move to make the debate public was already attention getting.

Then there was my methodology. One can make a public split with an organization in many ways—via press release or by making a speech or by speaking with a journalist. I bypassed all those options and used Twitter:

*I'm thinking of leaving Keidanren. What do you all think?*

With that, I set the business world buzzing.

In just a handful of characters, I accomplished a great deal. I made public my views on energy policy. I revealed my dispute with the leadership of Keidanren on this critical national issue. And I made a significant statement regarding the use of social media. I was not a teenager tweeting about the latest music or fashion item; I was a CEO of significant standing. My use of social media made my position on the medium clear: It was not just for teenagers anymore. It was a force in the leadership of the global business community.

So many of the leaders in social media technology have adopted cute names for their products—names like Twitter and Mixi and Stickies and HootSuite. These diminutive names belie the power of the tools. Social media are not child's play. The industry is a force for change in business, in politics, and in all things global. At Rakuten, we place great emphasis on the use of social media and are not taken in by the sweet branding imagery. These are serious tools for serious work.

## SOCIAL MEDIA AS A BUSINESS TOOL

Rakuten was already on a meteoric rise when we noticed a potential speed bump ahead. When we began our business, we were unique in our use of the Internet. We were out in front of the pack and this was bringing us great success. But a threat was looming. Eventually, we knew, we could be copied.

E-commerce is a business in which copycats are rampant. It is relatively easy to see what your competition is doing and to copy it quickly. If one runs a brick-and-mortar company, it might be more difficult for a competitor to study the details of your business and come into your space with a cheaper, flashier copy of your offering. Not so in e-commerce. The power of the Internet is such that great online businesses are quickly transparent to all.

This was certainly the case in consumer e-commerce. In the early days, the pioneers had the space to themselves. But others quickly caught on. And with that competition, some truisms of e-commerce began to take shape. It became clear that success in e-commerce rested on three critical elements:

1. Convenience. A site needed to be open and available to do business anytime, anywhere. All items for sale had to be available at all times. Shoppers quickly learned to expect and demand 24/7 retailing and rejected any e-commerce provider that could not live by those rules. Outages and out-of-stock products were considered signs of a poor business, and reputations were speedily tarnished by even short-term disruptions in availability.

2. Value. While consumers did not always demand the lowest price, they demanded what came to be known as a "best" price—a price that was reasonable, in line with industry standards, and comparable to what might be available on other e-commerce sites.

3. Security. An e-commerce site had to deliver a safe and worry-free transaction. Consumers needed to feel confident in entrusting their credit card numbers to the site. They had to have confidence that their order would be handled swiftly and with little fuss or disruption.

The problem with these three critical elements is that over time, many e-commerce sites were able to achieve them. While in the early days it was notable if your e-commerce site was always available or trouble free, as time went on consumers came to expect this as a basic right of e-commerce shopping.

At Rakuten, we could see this coming—a time when all major e-commerce players would be able to reliably offer the three critical elements of convenience, value, and security, perhaps in as soon as five to ten years. What would then differentiate the Rakuten retailer? How could the small and midsize merchants in our roster hope to attract customers when every e-commerce player could basically offer the same level of service?

To deal with this threat, we turned to social media. We did so early, when most were using social media as an entertainment element rather than a true business tool. It was still considered experimental by many when we sought to incorporate it into the overall Rakuten system. But we knew it was necessary, since the generalization of the e-commerce experience was coming. It was only a matter of time.

We call our social media program *Tencho No Heya*. Translated, this means "the store manager's room." What we have sought to do with social media is create a virtual space in which the individual store manager could "live." This is a space in the Rakuten platform that allows the merchant to communicate with customers—past, present, and future. Using social media, we have given the store manager a voice in the Rakuten shopping experience.

This is not a space for random social-media comments. Instead, we instruct our merchants to consider social media use for three key efforts:

- To highlight the attractiveness or his or her individual store
- To embrace customers and provide a dedicated space for them
- To manage e-commerce activities efficiently and effectively

## SOCIAL MEDIA AND MERCHANTS

We encouraged merchants to post information that would help the customer develop more of a personal relationship with the store manager—as if this person were not a virtual e-commerce seller but instead a neighborhood merchant in the customer's town. To do that, we told merchants, you must post more than just the basic information about your product and services. You must get personal.

Merchants have responded. Many, for example, post product-development diaries. They let customers in on the process of creating a new product for sale. This allows customers to see what goes into making a product and allows them to see the dedication and investment of the merchant.

Other merchants use the platform to tell the unique stories of their particular product line. One merchant, a seller of eggs, posted a daily test he gave to his eggs to determine their quality. His eggs, he posted, were the best available anywhere. To prove it, he photographed an egg with a tooth-pick stuck in the middle. The toothpick did not fall over, the merchant pointed out, which indicated the superior quality of his eggs. He conducted this test and posted the results daily—a daily testament to his product and one that drew fans as they logged on to see how well his eggs would perform on any given day.

This was a unique, engaging way for the merchant to reach out to potential customers. Certainly, a merchant could simply say: "My eggs are the best quality." Instead, he said: "Watch while I demonstrate that my eggs are the best quality." The use of social media made the ordinary product statement more interesting and more engaging for the customer. Soon, the merchant had back orders for his eggs—a remarkable achievement, since eggs are widely available and certainly do not need to be sourced online. Yet customers were convinced, in part due to the merchant's smart use of social media, that these particular eggs were superior. The story of the eggs had been told with skill and credibility. The ordinary eggs in the supermarket had no personal story to go with them—they could not compete.

Other merchants have used social media postings to let customers follow them on product-buying trips. These trip diaries allow the customer a chance to go behind the scenes and see how materials are sourced. It's also a great way for shoppers to understand how what they buy is now connected to the world around them. Customers have followed along online while Rakuten merchants sourced materials within Japan, traveled to other countries to find out about new materials and new products, and allowed readers to see how even a small merchant interacts with the global economy.

Merchants have used social media tools to put a human face on the e-commerce experience. Often postings are used to introduce customers to new employees, or to update them on the progress merchants are making with certain products. This helps build the feeling of closeness that a customer might expect in a neighborhood shop, which has often proved elusive in an e-commerce environment.

Naturally, these personalized moments are combined with more traditional merchant communications, such as news about store events, information about new products, and detailed descriptions of the products for sale. Social media postings allow Rakuten merchants to combine traditional retail communication with more personalized and unique information that makes customers feel closer to them.

Critical to the Rakuten social media strategy is a diversity of platforms. Companies get themselves into trouble when they embrace a single tool. In today's Internet environment, all tools are constantly in danger of becoming obsolete. Even while a great new tool is enjoying success and popularity, there is someone, somewhere, in an R&D lab working feverishly to create something even better. This is particularly true in a space such as social media, which has attracted so many creative and entrepreneurial-minded individuals. I have even experienced this in my own use of social media. While Twitter has served me well, I am now moving on to new social-media platforms. No one social-media strategy is forever. The space is uniquely fluid.

For that reason, diversity of social-media platforms is important. I never wanted Rakuten merchants to be tied to one platform—they must use many and assume that they will use even more in the future. This is the best mind-set for success. We did a study of our merchants in 2012 and found they were successfully using Facebook, Mixi, Google+, and Twitter. We created a screen by which our merchants could access these many tools easily and efficiently. The result is that Rakuten merchants not only use one kind of social media, but they also participate in the full landscape of social media options and will be able to do so even as newcomers enter the space. In technology, there is always a new invention right around the corner. To be successful, you must embrace what is available now and also be ready for whatever is coming—because something is surely coming.

As part of our training of merchants, we encourage them to consider the social media postings not as one-way communications but as a part of conversations. Technology allows merchants not just to deliver information but also to engage in a back-and-forth with the customer—and indeed, customers have come to expect this level of personalized communication. When a customer posts a review, for example, the merchant is encouraged to comment and reply. Other customers can also post their comments and replies. This creates reasons for the customer to be present on the bulletin board—to interact with the merchant and also to interact with other customers. By providing this communications space, the merchant has strengthened his relationship with his customer.

When we created tools for our merchants to use, we looked for ways that their use of social media would provide an ongoing stream of benefit to their business. We made sure, for example, that our tools allowed not just for text communication but also for the display of visual information. So much of what Internet users experience online is visual, and we made sure Rakuten merchants could also communicate in this way. Even when a merchant posts information that is not related to stores, visuals from the store are still visible, providing a quick visual cue for the customer even when the text is not directly selling.

We also created an article display widget to help merchants better spread the word of their efforts. When merchants post articles to their own Tencho No Heya Plus+ platform, the article title is automatically listed in the article display widget. This not only gets more readers for the article but also helps improve the merchant's performance in organic search results.

Finally, we created tools that allowed our merchants to see clearly how their social media efforts were performing and to give them the opportunity to adjust for maximum efficiency. Rakuten's visual-analysis tools let merchants review their page views and unique users. It allows them to track the performance of certain key words and also sorts the demographic information of customers by age and gender.

As part of our training, we encouraged Rakuten merchants to understand which social media tools were best used at different points in the customer cycle. Each merchant may have different needs at different times and we helped them understand the value of social media tools to attack different customer service issues. To attract consumers—to gather them in—posting articles is a tool to create buzz. To make a sale, a merchant might turn to posting comments to communicate directly with customers and address specific issues. Once customers have made a sale, the process of delivering omotenashi—superior and personal customer service—is at hand. For this, the tool of bulletin boards, which allow for long, detailed, ongoing conversations, may come into play. Merchants are encouraged to understand that not all social media tools are created equal, and it takes thoughtful consideration to know when each tool may be appropriate.

With all these tools, we armed our merchants to stay ahead of the inevitable commoditization of e-commerce. By the time most e-commerce sites were achieving the basic standards of convenience, best pricing, and security, Rakuten merchants were already adept at using social media to maintain a personalized, unique experience that could not be copied by the competition. No matter how many egg sellers come online, our Rakuten egg merchant will still have a lead because he has used social media to tell his story, create a conversation, and embrace his customers in a unique and compelling way. Another may set up shop and compete with him on convenience, price, and security. But that competitor will also have to compete with our merchant on story. In that respect, our merchant has a head start.

We don't require our merchants to use social media tools, however. Many come to the Rakuten marketplace with little experience in e-commerce, and even learning to use the computer is a big step. The fast-moving world of social media may seem even more complex and out of reach. But we consider it our job to make the tools available and the training to go with them. We design them for beginners and make sure to emphasize how leveraging social media can increase sales. It's not about forcing a particular way of doing business on to the merchant; it's about making the latest and best opportunities for success available to them. When you look closely at the experiences of successful Rakuten merchants, it is not uncommon to find individuals who started out with few technical skills yet quickly mastered the art of social media communication. When we show them what is possible, they respond with enthusiasm.

I am confident in our social media strategy in part because it is such an integral part of our business. Our passion for the personal story has always been part and parcel of the Rakuten process. In many ways, we were following this path of sharing conversation and personal stories even before most of the social media tools emerged. When we first began, we were often called "a blog with a shopping cart attached." This was a reference to our point of emphasis. Rakuten was first a gathering place for individuals and their stories and conversations. Attached to that important process were our marketplace and our shopping services. This is the theme that distinguished us from the Amazons and other "vending machine" systems of e-commerce development. We were never interested in creating a uniform, faceless experience. We were always interested in the individual and the story that individual was ready to tell the world. Because we have always stressed the storytelling process, as social media tools have emerged we have been able to embrace them with confidence and excitement. It is as if we had been waiting for them to arrive.

Do social media pose a threat to us? Some suggest that a virtual marketplace such as Rakuten is threatened by the rise of social networking. Certainly, there are new tools that let you search for products across multiple sites, and those could be seen as competitors. But I see social networks less as a threat and more as potential collaborators that will ultimately benefit all. The key is not to take a defensive stance and build a wall around your business, but to reach out and make positive connections that create a better experience for all involved. We work with social networks such as Facebook. We have released our API to them. We do this because we see how both a company like Facebook and a company like Rakuten could benefit from working together. Social networks are not in the retail business. They are in the communication business. They do not want to get into the day-to-day work of managing business deals or handling deliveries. That is what we in e-commerce do. By playing our respective roles well, we can all make our customers even happier.

Going forward, we will focus on the ways in which social media are evolving and how we can continue to be part of that global trend. Social networking sites such as Facebook and Foursquare offer powerful word-of-mouth marketing opportunities for Rakuten merchants as we expand our global position. Social media are widely used in Thailand and Indonesia, for example, making social networking an efficient way for Rakuten merchants to connect with new consumers in new countries.

Also, we must continue to hone our own technical capabilities so that we can lead our merchants to the best possible use of these tools. For example, as Facebook expanded in popularity, we developed our own specific functions for the social network. These were fun, and they allowed merchants to get very creative with the platform. But just offering functions is not enough—we also have to offer the education and support they need to make social media tools effective and attractive. There are lots of storeowners who still have no idea what Facebook is, and I believe Rakuten's strength as a hub is to help merchants understand the opportunity and the connection between these new tools and greater sales.

## THE FUTURE OF THE INTERNET

One of the most exciting and challenging aspects of the Internet revolution is that we're still so early in its story. The changes that it will bring to business, to society, and to human existence are only just beginning to emerge. In the history books, the advent of the Internet will be as dramatic as the Industrial Revolution or the invention of the automobile. This will take many years to play out and we are only in the very first stages of its impact.

The vastness of this impact is both good and bad. On the one hand, it will create even more competition for all of us. When we had to compete only within the boundaries of our nations, we had a defined challenge. Today, we compete with everyone who has joined the global community via the Internet. And as the Internet and broadband access expand throughout the world, that expansion will bring even more businesses into the global marketplace. This is good for those of us who want to find new markets, and also bad because it will mean many more competitors. As we like to say in Rakuten, "the pro is the con."

Still, those challenges bring with them a chance to reinvent many industries. In the near term, the Internet will remake television, advertising, and merchandising. Soon, it will revolutionize education. Eventually, all industries will be touched by the technology, and new possibilities for collaboration, speed, and joy will become as real for them as they are for me today.

## TRY THE RAKUTEN WAY

- Consider that the Internet is much more than a vending machine.
- Understand that the Internet is still evolving, still giving us new communications platforms such as social media.
- Create a vision for the Internet that allows for continued evolution, continuous communication, and empowerment.

# SEVEN

# REWRITING THE RULES OF E-COMMERCE

## DISCOVERY SHOPPING

It is never too early to rewrite the rules of any system. Although we often approach long-standing traditions when we look to shake things up, I don't believe there should be any sacred cows. Even if rules are relatively new, if change can make them more efficient or effective, it's time to act.

This is certainly the way we approached e-commerce. When we got into the industry, it was quite new; even now, it's barely twenty years old. New technologies and new ways of doing business emerge every day. It is an industry in constant flux and evolution. Still, the rise of a few alpha retailers, such as Amazon, led many companies to embrace an initial set of "rules," even in this fluid industry.

We did not, and we still don't. In this chapter, we will examine how our resistance to the "rules" of e-commerce has created a path to success not only for us but also for our vendors and clients as well.

The rules of e-commerce may be new. But there is always room for improvement.

## HOW PEOPLE SHOP

In the neighborhood where I grew up, you can walk down the street and find many types of merchants selling to the local customers. In one direction, you will find a fish market run by an individual owner we have all known for many years. Farther down the same road, you will find a supermarket. That establishment is newer, owned by a company rather than by an individual. It also sells fish, sometimes at prices much lower than those of the sole proprietor.

Yet both sellers make a living in the neighborhood. How is that possible, when they compete head-to-head selling the same product, and the supermarket is almost always cheaper? If you believe the current thinking in the business of consumer marketing today, cheap will always win, and anyone looking for fish in my old hometown will use only the supermarket.

But that doesn't happen. Some small merchants are hurt by the advent of a supermarket, but not all of them are. There is room in the economy for these smaller players. That's because they provide something additional to the customer that the big market can't copy: a human face.

Perhaps the biggest, most entrenched rule we challenge as a company is that price trumps all. It is easy to see how this "rule" evolved. In recent decades, many retailers have soared to spectacular heights by offering lower prices. Walmart is the premier example. More recently, Amazon is another. As the business world watched these companies succeed, it's natural that they would assume that price is the primary reason people shop in one venue rather than another.

At Rakuten, we never embraced this assumption. Certainly, customers care about getting a good price, a fair price. They do not want to blindly hand over money without receiving a proper good or service in return. But in our experience, the idea that money is the only impetus for consumer behavior never rang true. We established and expanded the Rakuten marketplace on the theory that there are many other motivators—among them, the human element. In this chapter, I will discuss how this human element has functioned and continues to function as a primary driver of consumer behavior. Our belief in and our commitment to this theme is perhaps the most important element that sets us apart from other e-commerce players. Many of the largest players have made a clear stand in the marketplace, offering price and efficiency as the only real competitive advantage. We believe the truth is far more nuanced and demands e-commerce providers that are willing to see and support that complexity.

## DISCOVERY SHOPPING

When I first got into this business, I had a vision for an e-commerce experience that was more than just cheap and efficient. I was looking for more than the vending-machine experience—put credit card in, get goods in return—which, while functional, seemed like not much fun. There had to be room for fun, I thought. And it did not have to be frivolous fun. It could and should be purposeful fun—fun as a driver of commerce.

In our early days, we called this "entertainment shopping," a process that not only got you the goods you needed but also provided you with a pleasant experience. We designed our site in a way that was playful and stimulating, and we encouraged our merchants to follow suit. Don't rush your shopper to the exit, we said. Welcome your shopper and share what is enjoyable and unique and entertaining about your business.

In many ways, this is a contrast in focus. We designed Rakuten to be shop-centric—a platform that encouraged and enabled consumers to discover different shops that might fit their needs. By contrast, many of our competitors are more product-centric—designed to help the consumer find a specific product. What's different about these two approaches? The Rakuten approach takes a longer view of the shop–shopper relationship. Our goal is to create a system by which shoppers get what they need at any given moment and then also have the opportunity to discover more that they might enjoy. The more standard e-commerce approach, on the other hand, focuses on getting the consumer the specific product at that moment. It's more of a search experience than a shopping experience. Efficient, to be sure, but hardly an avenue for discovery—only for acquisition. In our mind, this limits the possibilities for both the shopper and the merchant. Discovery, we've found, creates the potential for additional sales and additional successful shopping trips.

To ensure this user experience would exist across our vast network of merchants, we had to allow for freedom and customization among our clients. We gave them the tools and the flexibility to design their sites in such a way that made them unique. This flexibility is vastly different from the site design of our major competitors. Vendors on the more rigid platform conform to the template. This is efficient, to be sure. It saves money and time. But is it fun? Is it entertaining? Does it inspire the customer to spend time browsing? Not really.

A Rakuten customer, on the other hand, comes to our site knowing he or she will never have the same experience twice. Quite the opposite. There are no "cookie-cutter" stores in our ecosystem. We celebrate their differences and we encourage our customers to expect a diverse selection as their right. Over the years, we codified our description of this experience. It could not be *only* entertaining—anything with flashy graphics or other new technology could be entertaining. Customers were not coming to us for pure entertainment. Rather, they were coming to discover. We had created a platform built for more than speed and efficiency. We had created a forum for discovery shopping.

## WHAT IS DISCOVERY SHOPPING?

Let's stop and think about this for a moment. What are the elements that make up a discovery shopping experience?

- People behind the screen: perhaps the most obvious element is the ability to "meet" and connect with the virtual merchant. Unlike their experience on other marketplace platforms, Rakuten merchants know their end customers. They can connect with them freely and exchange information, and merchants have control of and access to the relationship. This allows them to be fully human to their customers, even if they only interact online.

- Community: a discovery shopping experience is one that draws information from a variety of sources, not just the vendor. In many cases, shoppers want to ask other shoppers what they think of the product or service. They may want to read comments, ask questions, or engage with other users before making a purchase. This is part of the discovery process, and Rakuten encourages and empowers its merchants to provide such forums. Rakuten stores often feature vibrant communities in which shoppers all over the world can talk to the merchant—and among themselves—about the goods for sale. By opening this multivoice conversation, we create more avenues of discovery for the shopper.

This social layer of the shopping experience is expanding rapidly, thanks to new technologies. While the very idea of a web-based forum was cutting-edge a few years ago, today shoppers expect to be able to connect through social media, using mobile devices if they prefer, and to engage in both word-based and visual conversations. Part of our mandate as we move forward is to remember that the shopper *wants* to be social and is constantly on the hunt for new technologies to make that happen. When we purchased the ebook company Kobo, one of the elements that attracted us was its commitment to the social aspects of reading. While our competitors provide technology that allows a single reader to enjoy a book, Kobo's technology allows that reader to connect with others who are also reading it. The eReader experience is enhanced by the opportunity to discover new friends, new conversations, and new layers to the book itself.

This commitment to the discovery aspect of e-commerce also came into play when we invested in Pinterest. This content-sharing service, which allows members to "pin" images, videos, and other objects to their pin board, is yet another example of the way shoppers are demanding a richer, more engaged e-commerce experience—one that displays emotion and entertainment rather than acting merely as a vending machine committed to low price and efficiency. Pinterest's appeal is rooted in emotional response. "Organize and share things you love," it invites its users. The opportunity to share with others and discover their suggestions in return is what fuels this and other curated shopping experiences. It's not just about speed or price. It's about the chance to discover new things to love.

As the platform provider, you must be willing to trust your clients and provide them with transparency and empowerment. Many of the early e-commerce providers failed because they tried to keep their merchants contained in a virtual mall. This system led to the downfall of many early projects. Doing the opposite of this failed strategy is what powered our start and continues to fuel our expansion. The world is full of creative, ambitious merchants ready to take their offerings to the global stage. To lead this diverse and voluminous group forward, Rakuten has committed to a process defined by empowerment and transparency. We believe in their ability to succeed.

## WHY DISCOVERY SHOPPING WORKS

To the untrained eye, discovery shopping may look like a losing strategy. How can something *less* efficient than its rival succeed? There are two reasons: First, humans like variety. People are not wedded to any one way of behaving. It's perfectly reasonable for an individual to want one experience one day and a different one the next. In fact, a world without variety quickly becomes boring. So discovery shopping naturally plays into the human desire for novelty. Think of it this way: I often walk through a park near my home. I have already found the quickest path through it. That's fine when I'm in a hurry. But I am not in a hurry every day. Sometimes I may wander from this efficient path to see what else is there for me. Perhaps I'll find that my first path is still my favorite. But I may come upon something new and wonderful by changing my route—opening myself up to the discovery process.

The same holds true for shopping experiences. When I'm in a hurry, I may be perfectly satisfied with a vending machine experience. But more often, I'm in the mood to browse. I would be very unhappy if my park offered only one path and didn't allow me to explore.

Secondly, humans like other humans. Recall the story about the two fish retailers in my hometown. Assuming the fish quality is similar, why would anyone choose the sole proprietor over the supermarket? One reason is the pull of human relationships. We may decide that we want to take our business to the small fish merchant because we like him. Perhaps he is courteous when we enter his shop. Perhaps he offers us individualized attention that we cannot find at the supermarket. Perhaps we know him from the neighborhood. But these human reasons are powerful. People don't buy goods from store shelves or computer screens. They buy from other people. Discovery shopping reassures us that shopping online need not wipe out the human-retailer relationship. It is still possible and desirable to create that relationship in a virtual environment.

In fact, this was the immediate concern when Internet shopping first rose to prominence—that we would lose this human experience, replacing it with a machine and a credit card. But Rakuten rewrote that "rule" even as it was born. As I said, it's never too early!

## FUN IS PROFITABLE

Our years in business have proven that our devotion to the human element of e-commerce is not incongruous. In fact, it's what propels many of our merchants to their greatest successes. When we look at some of Rakuten's leading merchants, we often find this element of fun at the root of their strong performance. Merchants who were able to see the potential for fun were the ones who first realized that the early rules of e-commerce were already ripe for rewriting.

Yonayona brewery is one of the oldest businesses in the Rakuten system. It debuted the year the marketplace first emerged—1997. It was a business born offline, opening its first shop in the 1990s when Japan was in the midst of a healthy microbrew boom. Yonayona, a Nagano-based craft ale brand, quickly enjoyed healthy sales throughout Japan.

But like many booms, it didn't last. By the mid-2000s, with the boom subsiding, the number of microbreweries across Japan had dropped dramatically, and so had Yonayona's sales.

What saved the company? E-commerce. CEO Naoyuki Ide realized early on that e-commerce was more than a vending machine. It was a platform for fun. With that, he joined Rakuten and set about servicing the company's enthusiastic online following.

"What I realized is that this is a service business as well," he says. "We make beer—but we serve our customers fun with it."

The Yonayona site includes blogs, photos, special offers, and other interactive content. "We actually have more people working on the site than we do salespeople," says Ide.

Now 70 percent of Yonayona's sales are online. What's more, online sales have lifted retail sales. Ide says that is because customers often pester their local supermarket to stock Yonayona after seeing it online.

Key to Yonayona's success is Ide's willingness to put a human face on his online sales. It's not unusual for him to wear a costume to Rakuten events; once he dressed as a shiny gold Yonayona robot and greeted crowds at an awards ceremony. One special campaign featured a competition for a case of beer specially delivered by Ide to the lucky winner. All was entertainingly documented online: journey, delivery, and impromptu drinking session.

"When we make beer at Yonayona we are very serious," says Ide, "but when we sell it we have fun."

## FUN IS FLEXIBLE

"Cheap" means only one thing. It means a low price. And "efficient" means only one thing. It means fast. But "fun" means many things to many different people, and when we focus on a goal of providing entertainment and enjoyment, we open many possible avenues of success for ourselves and our partners.

By encouraging our merchants to focus on the best way to entertain customers while shopping, we encourage them to continuously experiment with new and exciting changes to their sites. One of our merchants, a fashion shop called Yumetenbo, credits Rakuten with teaching it the "ABCs of the online business." But all we really did was teach its management to embrace the constantly evolving elements of online shopping that their customers found fun.

Yumetenbo began its relationship with Rakuten in the late 1990s. Its managers were new to e-commerce. CEO Takahiro Oka attended Rakuten University to learn the skills necessary to compete—not so much technical skills as a mind-set open to the best process for e-commerce. He learned that success was not about who could make the fastest or cheapest website. "One of the most important things I learned was to make us different," he says.

To make this happen, Yumetenbo invested time and money in its website's visual imagery, investing in fashion shoots and new video offerings daily. And it made sure to keep pace with its customers as they discovered new technology. While early sales came via the desktop computer, almost a decade later over half its sales now come from cell phones. And as customers branch out into the next generation of new media, Yumtenbo will be right there with them.

This does not mean Yumetenbo rejects the other rules of e-commerce. Speed, a hallmark of the major e-commerce players, is also a big part of Yumetenbo's mission. Since Japan has one of the most colorful and fast-paced young fashion scenes in the world, keeping up is a constant race against the clock. It now takes as little as three months to design and manufacture a new item—and Yumetenbo introduces three hundred of these each month. A fully equipped photo studio at the company headquarters means that Oka can quickly order reshoots of the merchandise based on customer feedback. Nothing is allowed to stall and become stale.

But Oka does not let the pressure to be fast keep him from remembering the main goal of his customer: to discover new and glamorous clothes. His store has become a favorite case study at Rakuten, and we emphasize the secret of his success over and over. He is not a vending machine. He provides an ongoing source not just of clothing but also of entertainment.

## THE POWER OF ENGAGEMENT

Ultimately, the reason this type of e-commerce works is engagement. To keep a customer coming back, online shopping must always make engagement a priority. In their short histories, e-commerce companies have learned that engagement is a more complex process than simply getting the customer's attention. It requires seizing that attention to build a more nuanced relationship—and, as technology evolves, ensuring that that relationship is sustained across all platforms, whether established or evolving.

The most successful e-commerce players know that engagement is a never-ending process of connection. You can't strive for a single moment of engagement. The connection with your customer must be forged and tended with every interaction. This is how a brick-and-mortar store functions.

Every time a customer enters, the merchant strives to make that customer happy. He will greet the customer, serve the customer's needs, and think later about how to reach out to that customer again and bring him back into the store in the future. It would never occur to him to make only one effort at engagement, then assume a relationship going forward.

The same efforts are necessary online. Merchants must consider each customer to be more than just a one-touch target. At Rakuten, this is our philosophy and we provide on-going support and teaching to our merchants to help them follow this plan. When our merchants use blogs and photos and video to connect with customers, they are doing more than flinging out advertising messages. They are creating an ongoing process of engagement, which creates a lasting, meaningful customer relationship. It does not wipe out the customer's chance to engage with retailers in brick-and-mortar stores. But it creates another way customers can experience that fun, human factor in this virtual environment.

This is why I am so certain that the vending machine model is limited in scope. There is no relationship with a vending machine. There is no human being to connect to. Indeed, the companies following the vending machine process are careful to construct a platform that strictly prohibits contact between original seller and end user. Each of those two parties knows only the vending machine platform; neither has direct contact with the other. Naturally, they have no relationship. The possibility for engagement is deliberately blocked.

This does not mean that shoppers reject the vending machine platform entirely. Many will try it for a variety of reasons: convenience, speed, or a lack of awareness of other options. But the hold that vending machine purveyor has on the customer is limited. Any relationship built on convenience leaves that customer open to wooing by another merchant. If another merchant comes along and shows the customer a way to shop online and have more fun, why should the customer stick with the vending machine? People like to buy from people. They always have. That's why marketplaces throughout human history have always been such vibrant, attractive places. They aren't just places to acquire necessities. They are locations where humans gather to interact, do business, and engage. The same human needs drive us when we engage in e-commerce. Even when facing a screen, we seek out humanity.

## THE FUTURE OF DISCOVERY

Even as dueling visions for e-commerce play out today, we must always be looking to the future. Naturally, the most desirable model is one that is not only profitable now but also will be profitable in the future.

This is where I believe the discovery model makes its most compelling case. Competing on efficiency and price alone is a zero-sum game. There is eventually an end point where you can no longer reduce the price or wring any more efficiency out of the process. You have done the best you can do. While that might please the customer in the moment, it will eventually grow stale. Even happy customers eventually want more. It is our nature as human beings to never be permanently satisfied. We are always optimistic that something better is coming just around the corner.

This is the mind-set that most favors the discovery model. Customers know the price of an item cannot drop forever, and delivery can never be instant for physical goods. So there is a limit to how happy you can make the customer under the price/efficiency model. Our discovery model, on the other hand, allows for a future. It promises that there is always something new coming. It allows us to embrace every new technology platform that evolves, such as mobile or social media. It allows us to continually change and add new elements to our offerings without confusing our brand message or shifting our mission.

The history of retail has always been one of discovery. It was the reason explorers set sail to find new markets and new products. It's the reason the method of getting goods and services to consumers is always changing. Nothing stays the same in retail because shoppers don't want the same. They want to discover. They always will.

As Rakuten expands across the globe, the debate over the competing visions for e-commerce will take on new urgency. Companies and customers will have to decide in which direction they want to go. A variety of leaders in the space will offer up their different platforms and visions. In the end, we believe that human history will win out. Our desire to discover is strong. When a business or technology offers us a new way to discover, we embrace it. As the customer looks for ways to travel the web, explore the cloud, and connect with goods and services all over the world, those of us who support and enhance that exploration will travel with them.

I doubt very much that anyone will cling to a vending machine. There is so much more for us to discover.

## TRY THE RAKUTEN WAY

- Envision your e-commerce goals not as a technical but as a new human expression. While new technologies are always emerging, consider each one not just for its technical abilities but for its potential to improve the human experience of shopping.
- Do not confuse search with shopping.
- Remember the tale of the two fish merchants. Price is not always the motivating factor.
- As human beings, we are driven to discover. Create a business that feeds this natural human impulse.

# EIGHT

# REWRITING THE RULES OF OPERATION

## SPEED, SPEED, SPEED!

Speed is a favorite topic of business leaders. When you hear them speak, it seems as if all of them see speed as vital. But when you look closely at their actions, speed gets more lip service than actual playing time. In truth, most business leaders worry more about making a high-profile mistake, and this makes them tentative—the opposite of speedy. This is a natural human impulse, so I find it even more necessary to make a point of my own desire for speed. I triple it to underscore my intention: Speed!! Speed!! Speed!! In many ways, speed is the secret weapon of the successful. When you look at a company or individual who has accomplished something extraordinary, speed is often at the root of their success. Here's an example from my own career that highlights the power of speed.

Back when I was first starting my own company, I got lots of unsolicited advice. Most people said: *Do not go into online retailing. The business model is flawed. Look at all the failed online retailers around the marketplace*, they said. *Online retail cannot succeed.*

In fact, online retailing was not suffering from a flawed business model at all. It was suffering from a lack of speed. There were many points in the online retail process that were just too slow to be successful. Website updates, for example, moved at a snail's pace. People believed then that website alterations had to be made by professional web designers—a process that took time and money. Because of this, retailers were slow to update their sites. It was not uncommon to see websites promoting Christmas items far into the New Year.

This made the websites look stale and boring. Compare it to a real-world shop window. If you walked past a window in January and it still had its old Christmas merchandise in the window, what would you think of the retailer? You certainly would not think, "This is a fashion-forward, cutting-edge merchant, and I must go inside to see what new and exciting wares he has to offer!" You would probably think, "Christmas decorations? Still? What is taking him so long to update his window?"

Online shoppers had this same reaction. Online retailers, to their eyes, seemed behind the times.

One of the first things I did when I got into online retailing was to attack this slowness that was dragging down the whole industry. I freed merchants from the idea that they had to hire expensive web designers to update their sites. I empowered them to make updates themselves. I gave them tools they could use. I gave them training on how to use them. I encouraged them to be as responsive and creative online as they were in their regular shop windows. Rakuten merchants were successful online not because they adopted a new business model—but because they were faster. Speed made the difference.

This early experience with the power of speed confirmed that it would be a core principle of my work and my company. I have made speed one of my five key principles. In this chapter, I will explore the concept of speed in more detail. I'll talk about what I really mean when I say "speed," and reveal the ways to encourage speed in individuals, companies, and even the larger society. Many things we think of as flawed in the world might be fixed with speed.

## WHAT IS SPEED?

Let's talk first about what I mean when I use the word "speed." There are actually two types of speed that I believe are critical to success: velocity and agility.

Velocity is the rate at which something happens. To gain speed, you must amp up velocity. In other words, the process, whatever it is, must unfold at a quicker rate. In the work

world, velocity is most often achieved through efficiency improvements—shortening meetings, decreasing the number of
copies made, reducing the number of people on a project. All
these make the original process slimmer, lighter, and therefore
faster. It's not a difficult concept to visualize. If you are walk-
ing down the street carrying an armload of packages, you will
move at one rate. If you can shed your burden, you will move
more quickly. Every athlete knows to choose the lightest possible gear to achieve maximum velocity.

In the workplace, it's not as simple as putting something
down or changing to lighter clothing. The "shedding" of extra weight must come through the elimination of wasted time
in the workday. We'll talk more specifically about how to do
that later in this chapter.

The second definition of speed is agility. This is the speed
at which you act after you have decided something. Agility
is especially useful when changing direction—both physically
and mentally. When a player needs to change direction on the
soccer field, agility will help him do this without stumbling.
The same is true in business. The decision to change direction
must be executed with agility—a quick and purposeful move.
Often, in business, we forget to hone agility. We allow our
anxiety over changing direction to slow the shift. On the soccer field, this slowness gives the opponent a chance to thwart
the athlete's efforts. In the work world, a lack of agility can
be similarly dangerous.

In my daily work, I strive to model these types of speed.
I am often encouraging staff to trim waste—particularly

practices that waste time. This is a process I engage in all the time, and it's a part of everyday work at Rakuten. I am always asking: Are there ways we can eliminate the wasting of time in that activity? Can we improve upon the process so that it is faster? Velocity is a constant priority.

At the same time, I am also always modeling agility. Whenever I start something new, I dive straight into it. I believe there is no point in worrying over your decision; all you can do is act. I run toward my goals. I believe my team works fastest when they are trying to catch up with me. This is one more way to bring everyone around me up to their top speed.

In many ways, my passion for speed was stoked by my time at Harvard Business School. There is no course on speed at Harvard, yet it is a constant theme across many of the topics taught there. So many subjects—from marketing and sales to technology and service—included speed as part of the lesson. This became a thread of connection for me as I moved through the curriculum. The greatest companies shared a passion for speed at all levels of execution. Whether it was assembling an automobile or designing a computer game or executing an online transaction, speed mattered. It was often the defining feature of the market leader, with the rest of the field racing to catch up.

## HOW TO ACHIEVE PERSONAL SPEED

How do you achieve speed? Once you an embrace the idea that speed is essential for you personally, there are many ways you can be faster. It is common for individuals to feel as though the speed at which they work is beyond their control, especially if they work for a large organization. They may think that their job is to move at the speed of the rest of the company.

I argue that this is an unfortunate misconception that drags down many companies and individuals. If you believe that speed is not your job, then it won't happen. Now imagine everyone in the organization assumes that speed is not his or her job. What happens then? A large organization simply lumbers along at the slowest common pace. You, as an individual, are dragged down by that lack of velocity and agility. Slow is a lose-lose situation for you and for your company. You should not put up with it.

Commit yourself—personally—to working with greater speed.

## SET GOALS

If you go on a trip without a set destination, you will meander. If, on the other hand, you set a goal, you will move much more directly toward your destination. Naturally, the direct route is faster. This is also true in business. If your goals are vague—or worse, if you have no real goals and just come into work every day with no long-term plan—you will move slowly. If you set goals for yourself, your speed will naturally increase.

Your goal need not be the quota handed to you by your supervisor. It can be a target you select for yourself. Indeed, the best goal you can set for yourself is one so high that achieving it would change your life. These are the goals that inspire us to our best and fastest work. If you are a mountain climber and you choose to scale a relatively small, safe peak, you will approach the mountain with a steady sense of purpose. But now imagine that you are standing at the base of the Matterhorn. The mountain looms above you, its tremendous scale dominating the horizon. This is a huge challenge, an audacious goal. To undertake it will stoke within you a rush of adrenaline—a mix of anxiety and excitement. It is a unique and powerful thrill that you have created for yourself, just by choosing this big goal. Now, with that adrenaline running through you, will you stroll at a leisurely pace to the mountain? No. You will be pumped full of excitement about your goal and it will naturally cause you to quicken your pace. You will have achieved speed simply by setting a big goal.

Here's an example of how goal setting worked for me. In the spring of 2000, I pledged to attain a business with a total gross transaction volume of one trillion yen ($12 billion). When I stated that goal, I got a lot of strange looks. Some said I was crazy. Others just shrugged off the statement and did not take it seriously. After all, in 2000, Rakuten was a company of only three billion yen ($35 million). One trillion yen was a huge, Matterhorn-size goal.

While others smirked, I felt the surge of excitement that comes with setting a big goal. I threw myself into this huge challenge. Not only did I achieve my goal, I achieved it faster than even I had imagined. Indeed, when I set the goal for my-self, I announced that I would retire when Rakuten achieved the one-trillion-yen mark. The goal helped inject speed into my business that even I did not expect. It was 2006 when the total transaction volume of Rakuten Group reached one tril-lion yen. I was nowhere near the age when I wanted to step out of the business world and retire. I had to take back my promise to retire! But it was a good reminder that a great goal can generate unprecedented speed.

## DON'T THINK, THEN ACT; THINK TO ACT

There is an unfortunate linear convention that has been ap-plied to thinking and acting in the business world. Many believe you must think first—focus all your energies on the thinking process—and then, when you are ready, act. This is a naturally slow process. Thinking, without a motivation to act, can put you in a permanent stall. You can think forever and never take action. Surely, we all know people who are always pondering their next moves and never take an actual step forward.

Because of this, one surefire way to incorporate more speed into your life is to reject this notion that thinking must come first and then be followed by action. Reject the linear process. Instead, embrace the idea that you can think *and* act, and then think and act some more. Resolve to embrace the simultaneous process.

Why is this faster? The reason is that by acting, you will actually improve your thinking. Thinking when you have no goal precludes thinking at its highest level. You feel no urgency, so you do not push your brain to its limits. On the other hand, if you are already in action, the impetus to think well is far greater. You are already in motion, so you must "think on your feet." This is a much greater intellectual challenge and stimulates the process itself. Action is food for thought.

This idea becomes obvious when one considers the process of learning a sport. Suppose you want to improve your tennis game. You can read many books about tennis. You can think a lot about how you would improve your technique and execution. All this can be done while you are sitting on the sidelines. Now, if I get you up, put a racket in your hand, and have you practice, how much faster will you improve? The real-world experience—the action of playing—will stimulate you to think of new ways to execute the improvements you've imagined. Action is what speeds improvement.

I'm not against deep thinking. It's a necessary and vital process. It goes without saying that those who are better thinkers will go further in this world. That said, if you seek to inject more speed into your execution, don't hold off on action while you think. Action doesn't stop your thinking process; it hastens and improves it.

This step requires some unusual courage. You are setting your process in motion and then committing to continue to think and refine it along the way. This is not the safe route. It may contain surprises. But it will also bring out your best and fastest thinking.

## CONSIDER THE PERSPECTIVES OF OTHERS

It may seem counterintuitive, but one way to increase speed is to see your job and the goals of your company not just from your own perspective, but from the perspectives of others around you. You might think such looking around is distracting and adds time to your workday, but I disagree. When you use only tunnel vision at work and see only your own tasks and your own responsibilities, you may be missing ways in which you can improve and work more quickly.

What I'm describing is not the bird's-eye view—a view from high above looking down. Instead, I think of it more as a four-dimensional view—a panoramic view in which you are on the ground level, but able to see all around you with equal clarity.

Here's an example. When I was a young recruit at IBJ, I worked in a division that dealt frequently with issues of currency. It was a job that required a lot of paperwork. In a company this large, you might be tempted to say there was nothing any one young employee could do to improve speed. After all, this was a massive organization with many layers of rules and regulations. It was not a start-up, where anyone might make a novel suggestion and carry it out.

Even so, I found a way to speed up my work, and I did so in part by looking around. Although I had my assigned tasks, I was not at work in a vacuum. There were other employees around me who were connected to my function. I began to take note of what they did. There were many women in the office, for example, who handled administrative functions. I observed them and I began to understand our little corner of IBJ not just from my perspective, but from theirs as well. Because I could now see the "big picture" of our department, I saw ways to handle the paperwork faster. I came up with ideas that made the women's administrative tasks easier. This made them happy and injected a positive mood into our work overall. I was able to inject speed into the workings of my department not just by doing my job well, but by understanding the needs of others around me and coming up with ways to help them do their jobs well.

Developing this panoramic perspective is critical to achieving substantial success. It's not just a question of speed—although that is important. When you can see your job as part of a larger whole, you learn to think comprehensively. You are less likely to be distracted by small or insignificant problems and will instead consider the broader themes and connections that develop in any business. When you can see your company comprehensively, you can make smarter decisions and provide more confident leadership.

## FALL IN LOVE WITH YOUR JOB

What does love have to do with your job? Everything. Love is a primary driver of speed on the job.

Think of it this way: Imagine you are running to catch a train. You want to catch the train, so you are running quickly. Perhaps you will jump over a small barrier or two and make your best effort to get there in time.

Now imagine your true love is on that train. How much faster would you run to catch that train? You would leap barriers that seemed insurmountable. You would push yourself to run faster than you've ever run before. You would spare no effort to catch that train and ride off into the sunset with your beloved.

So, what if you could find that kind of love and attach it to your job? If you fall in love with your job, it stands to reason that you will approach it with more speed than you would in a more moderate emotional state. Love makes people do the extraordinary.

This is not an easy concept to embrace. Many people will say it is impossible to love one's job. Perhaps you are not in your "dream" job. Perhaps you wished you worked for another company or that you had a higher rank or that you made more money. That is fine—everyone should aspire to greater things in life. These goals, as I've said, can be inspirational. But just because you hope to advance or improve eventually does not mean you can't fall in love with your job today. You simply have to believe that this is possible and, indeed, necessary. Put your mind to it. Find the elements of your job that you can be passionate about. If your job involves a lot of routines and paperwork, look for ways that you can make it into a game. Challenge yourself to see how much faster you can complete your tasks without making a mistake. Just because your employer has not seen fit to frame your job in a way that is challenging and entertaining does not mean you can't do this for yourself.

Set goals for yourself and then challenge yourself to come up with innovative solutions. If your solutions work, bravo. If they do not, revisit the innovation process. When you change the way you think about your job—from a chore to a landscape for innovation—you open the possibilities for happiness and even love. When you love your job, you will race toward it every day, as the lover runs for the train. You will not even notice the greater speed at which you travel. It will come naturally as you pursue your emotional goal.

## HOW TO ACHIEVE CORPORATE SPEED

We have focused thus far on ways you, personally, can improve your own speed and perhaps the speed of those near you. The next question is: Can this commitment to improving speed be applied on a larger scale—company wide rather than just person by person? My experience leading my own company leads me to answer yes. It is possible not just to improve speed in one's own life and work. It is possible to lead for speed.

### ATTACK WASTE

This is part of my ongoing effort to improve speed. I am on a constant hunt for ways in which waste can be removed from the Rakuten business process. Perhaps the most famous of our company-wide efforts has been the Rakuten Meeting System. I noticed, as our company grew, how much time was being devoured by meetings. At these meetings, much of the time was spent with each participant speaking about what he or she was doing and bringing the other meeting participants up to date. At one point, I was sure that 90 percent of meetings was spent on these updates, leaving 10 percent for actual work to take place.

This was not speedy.

I couldn't help but think that this problem with meetings was not just my problem, but a much bigger drag on productivity. In my mind, I ran this math: If there are twenty million employees in Japan and each person spends one hour a day in meetings (and that is a very conservative number) we are looking at twenty million hours times five days a week times fifty-two weeks. A total of 5.2 billion hours! If that time were cut in half, it would free up 2.6 billion hours. That potential time savings was just too good to pass up.

I tried an experiment. I began to require that all materials for any meeting be distributed electronically to all participants by five P.M. the preceding day. Because everyone had the materials in advance, all the time we usually devoted to explanation and presentation could be cut. We could devote the meeting time to addressing perhaps the one or two items on the distributed materials that required additional explanation. Then we could move to actually making decisions and moving forward. Meeting times shrank drastically. Meetings that used to take one hour now took ten minutes. As everyone grew accustomed to creating and distributing materials, some meetings became unnecessary altogether, thanks to online communication such as instant-messenger apps like AIM or Netscape Communicator and internal social networks like Yammer.

Not all meetings can be streamlined, but many can. In fact, as we instituted the Rakuten Meeting System across the company, we found substantial savings. When you ask for speed in a regular office function, such as a meeting, you may be amazed at what's possible. It's simply that no one bothered to ask for it in the past.

With this in mind, I am always on the lookout for waste. When I am presented with a timeline for a project, I look at the process and the steps and try to find ways to save time. I suggest: Can you skip this step? Can you combine these processes? When you remove wasted activity, you improve speed.

## SET SPEED-ENHANCING DEADLINES

There is an art to setting deadlines so that it encourages the greatest possible speed from employees. When I set a deadline, I look for this sweet spot that will encourage the maximum productivity without producing so much anxiety that everyone is paralyzed.

If you set a deadline that is too close ("We will launch this new product next week!"), some of your employees may not bother. They may simply view it as hopeless and fail to try.

Then again, if you set a deadline that is too far off ("We will launch this new product in ten years"), you fail to inspire. Many will think, "Oh, I will not even be here when that happens."

When you set a deadline, you need to make it close enough so that everyone feels some anxiety. An individual who feels no sense of danger at all will not be inspired to greatness.

## DON'T OBSESS OVER PERFECTION; ACT AND IMPROVE

One major obstacle to speed on a corporate level is a focus on perfection. While of course it is important to strive for excellence at all levels, sometimes this passion for perfection can hold up the process in ways that hurt the company and the consumer. To allow for speed, you must, as a leader, be open to the fact that kaizen is a fact of life. You will launch a product or service. It will be as close to perfect as you can make it at that moment, but you will commit to continuing improvements as you move forward. If you wait for perfection, you may never launch at all. Whom does that stalled process serve?

As we mentioned earlier, one of the best practitioners of this launch-and-improve ethic is Microsoft. You can see it even in the way the company names its products—adding "7" and "8" as improvements are made and new versions of the product make their way to users. Some criticize Microsoft for this process. They make fun of the way that the company is constantly working to fix bugs and improve on products already in the marketplace. But this process is in fact the reason Microsoft is so successful. The company does not wait around, pondering every last detail, leaving its customers waiting and waiting for an upgrade. Instead, Microsoft acts boldly and with speed. It rolls out its product and remains engaged and committed to making improvements. Who cares if a product has multiple iterations? They're a sign of a company that values kaizen and uses the mind-set of improvement to achieve speed.

As a leader, it's important to communicate this tolerance for fixing a product or service "on the fly." Some employees may hold back, fearing that if they launch anything less than perfection, they will be punished. If you value speed, you must be clear to your staff that you want this speedy behavior to happen and that you acknowledge and expect that it will mean follow-up to fix flaws as they become apparent.

## CREATE POSITIONS THAT SUPPORT SPEED

One way leaders fail is when they demand speed but fail to provide the necessary tools for employees to carry it out. Sometimes these are physical tools, such as software or machinery. But sometimes they are human tools. As you run a company or division or team, look for ways that a human being, deployed in a unique way, can improve speed.

Here's an example from the Rakuten headquarters. As part of our "speed" promise, we made a goal that every individual who filled out our online form requesting information from a Rakuten mall representative would get a phone call from us within two minutes.

Two minutes is a very small window of time. It is a big demand. To attain that goal and to create a system by which we could do it over and over again, we deployed a unique tool— a human tool. We hired an individual whose only job was to place the two-minute phone call. That's all that person was responsible for. We did not burden our existing staff with this additional demand for speed. We hired a new employee so that it was possible for this new level of speed to be achieved.

## LOOK FOR BOTTLENECKS

Just as I am always on the lookout for waste, I am always on the lookout for bottlenecks. These can be processes that have outlived their usefulness and now just add time. They can be policies that were once critical but are now not necessary. They can even be physical—literal bottlenecks in the smooth workings of the company.

I remember a bottleneck we encountered when we moved our offices from Roppongi to Shinagawa City. Everything seemed to move smoothly—except on Mondays when we had our full-staff meeting at the start of the day. Every employee was required to attend this meeting, and therefore Monday mornings found thousands of employees trying to cram into the lobby elevators to get to this meeting on time. It took thirty minutes for everyone to take their seats.

When I saw this, I was furious. By my calculations, if each employee was losing thirty minutes, the whole company was losing 2,500 work hours that day. How could we demand speed and have our employees standing in line all morning to get into an elevator? It was unacceptable.

We attacked the problem by addressing the bottleneck. The answer, it turned out, was to reset the elevators. Quite a bit of time was being lost as the elevators stopped on every floor, both up and down. It was like boarding a local train and stopping at every station along the way—frustrated passengers elbowing their way in and out of crowded cars.

I decided that in our twenty-three-story building, the elevators would stop only at 1, 2, 3, 5, 7, 10, 13, 14, 17, and

21. Stairs would be easily accessible to travel between the remaining floors. We installed new panels on the elevator with only those buttons. We made exceptions, of course, for the disabled. But as a rule, employees were asked to use the elevator to travel only to those designated floors and use the stairs to access others.

The results: Time spent waiting for an elevator in Rakuten Tower dropped to five minutes. We raised the productivity of workers. We reduced the stress of elbowing through crowds to get to a meeting on time. Rather than accept the bottleneck, we attacked it.

## MEASURING FOR SPEED

Many companies fear speed because they fear making a mistake. At a high rate of speed, they worry that activities will spin out of control. Errors will be made. Opportunities will be missed in the blur of motion.

It's not an unreasonable fear. Speed can make it more difficult to spot key events as they unfold. But slowing down is not the answer to this challenge. We face the challenges created by speed with another strategy. We deploy a policy of metrics and measurement.

Too often, measurement is viewed not as an activity of speed, but an activity of slower, methodical work. We take the opposite view. At Rakuten, we measure everything, not in an attempt to slow down and take a more methodical look, but rather to keep a close eye on fast-moving events. When a company is moving rapidly, metrics are crucial so that a concrete picture of the business is visible at all times. It never becomes a fast-moving blur. For this reason, our passion for measurement and our passion for speed go hand in hand.

How do we make that happen without sacrificing either speed or accuracy?

## WE MEASURE ALL THE TIME

Measurement of even the smallest daily activities is one of the ways Rakuten has made its "lucky" rise. Many look at our company and say we were lucky. I know that what really moved us forward were incremental improvements—small, daily improvements. How do I know this? Because we measured everything all the time.

It is not enough to simply work diligently every day. Just be a little more efficient today than you were yesterday, and just a little more efficient tomorrow than you were today. No matter how high a mountain a climber aims to summit, he must start by putting one foot in front of the other. In terms of business, even a 0.01 percent improvement is fine. If you make a 0.01 percent improvement each day, after a year, you will be 44 percent better at what you do. Part of achieving that improvement is keeping track of the improvements. Measurement is a natural part of the improvement process.

## WE MEASURE RISK

It's not enough to measure just forward progress. To make a smart decision, you must also be able to measure risk. "Risk" is a word that is almost always partnered with the word "avoidance." This is a mistake when it comes to business. Often it is the individual willing to face risk who will be successful. If you look at the history of great companies, you will find an army of great risk takers.

The key is to understand precisely the type and size of the risk you face. This is a type of measurement exercise. You are attempting to quantify the risk you face by understanding its numbers.

We faced this type of situation early in the history of Rakuten when we first began our marketplace. The idea of an Internet shopping mall was already understood, and there was a demonstrated history of failure in Japan and other large nations. So how did we approach this clear and present risk?

My approach was not to be intimidated by the risk but to work to understand the size and scope of it—precisely—in order to make the best possible plans. The biggest risk I faced at that time was the possibility that the Internet would not spread as fast as I had predicted. The speed of proliferation that we saw in 1997 was not sufficient to attract enough customers to our marketplace. The initial business model depended upon the Internet spreading throughout the world at a rapid pace. There was always the possibility of going bankrupt if the Internet did not spread as quickly as I had predicted.

In order to deal with this risk, we set the fee for opening a shop on Rakuten's marketplace at fifty thousand yen (about $500) and we asked storeowners to pay for half a year's service up front. This meant that even if the Internet did not spread as fast as expected, we would still be able to keep a minimum cash flow. At the same time, we kept our capital investment and employee head count low. By keeping our scale low, we would be better able to wait, if need be, for the Internet to catch on widely. So our approach to risk was done not with bravado and bravery, but with precision and care. We worked to fully understand the size and type of the risk we faced, and we developed a plan to deal with it even in the worst-case scenario. We measured our risk and prepared an appropriate response.

## WE MEASURE TO PREDICT THE FUTURE

Perhaps metrics will not allow you to see into the future exactly, but you can still come up with several likely scenarios. To do this well requires not just smart forecasting but also smart data collection. The task of measuring how far we have come yields the data we need to predict where we might be going. Again I go back to my early days starting the Rakuten marketplace. I had set my price for new merchants low—and then I had to make predictions for the future. I did not have the power to envision the one true future, but I did have the ability to work out likely scenarios. Looking at Internet activity as it was at that time gave me the numbers I used to give my best forecast for the future.

## WE CRAFT OUR OWN TOOLS AND PROCESSES: THE MIKITANI CURVE

Quality is fostered or destroyed by 0.5 percent improvements. I encourage everyone in my organization to do their best—and then do 0.5 percent more. It's this last effort that pushes good products to best products.

Whether it is televisions or cars or rice cookers, manufacturers exert great effort to make sure their products are the best. The same is true for sales, your local café, restaurants, and each store in the Rakuten marketplace. Everyone is working their hardest to be the best.

Still, there are often obvious differences between one product or service and its nearest competitor. It is often clear that one product is good and the other is simply the best. Often the difference between good and best is so small, it's almost immeasurable. *Almost.* Because of course, if carefully measured, the difference can be revealed.

Suppose you have a piece of cotton fabric and a piece of silk. Which is softer? You can tell just by feeling them. However, if you examine the surface threads, the difference between the sizes of each thread may be less than 0.1mm. Between pieces of silk and cotton or even between two pieces of cotton, you can tell the difference in quality by feel alone. When you translate the differences into numbers, they may be close to zero. The smallest numerical difference may result in a substantial final result. The difference between cotton and silk. The difference between good and best.

Set this metric for yourself—the final 0.5 percent effort. This is the basis for what I call the Mikitani Curve. The last step is always the most important. It is in the last 0.5 percent of effort that you put into a job that improves everything. Be conscious of this metric and create a system to ensure that you always make this final effort. The very last bits of effort can improve the subjective quality of a product rapidly along a pattern not unlike a quadratic equation.

## APPLYING METRICS FOR SPEED

Measurement tactics can produce speed only when the results are applied in day-to-day operations. Here's how we do that.

### WE READ TRENDS BY THE NUMBERS

Sales, profitability, break-even points, organizational profits, shares, prices, customer figures—business is full of numbers.

Learning to read these numbers is an absolute requirement for management.

Numbers are facts. They do not lie to you or try to tell you what you want to hear. There are no more reliable tools to help you understand the details of your business.

Some may argue that numbers do, in fact, lie. A suspicious investment business will often create seemingly trustworthy graphs and calculations. In those circumstances, it may appear that numbers lie. But in fact, a closer examination shows that the numbers, if read correctly, would have told investors the truth.

The real reason numbers seem to lie is that sometimes the individual may misunderstand what they're actually saying. I'm not talking about "cooked" books or instances when someone is openly lying. That's a different situation. Most often, people are misled by numbers because of a problem in their own comprehension.

In order to read numbers correctly, you need to develop your ability to connect numbers to reality. You could also call this the ability to imagine bigger and better things by looking at numbers. If you do not have this skill, it does not matter how fast you are at calculations or how good you are at remembering numbers.

If you want to improve your ability to read numbers, you should start by chasing after changing statistics.

At Rakuten, all employees send daily reports to their superiors. We have made it so that the many figures received in each section each day are organized and sent to me. In one day, I receive a book five centimeters thick—all the numbers of the business of that day.

Just by looking at the numbers, you can see not only what is happening in your own business but also in the world around it. Numbers illuminate the circumstances as well as the results of a company in business. Ability to understand these numbers is the ability to understand where your business is right now—and where it might go tomorrow.

## WE USE MEASUREMENT TO SPEED INNOVATION

Finally, there is one more way we leverage the measurement process to move us more quickly toward our goals. We use measurement in pursuit of innovation. Far too many consider innovation a "dreamy" process, one that is tied to pure creative thinking. In fact, great innovation is inspired by dreams and launched by a structured, considered process. Measurement plays a key role in launching the biggest dreams. It provides the foundation for the possibility.

Develop metrics to measure your intuition.

Is there a metric for imagination? We think so.

Let's say you forget to bring a book along on your commute one day. You are suddenly inspired to open a bookstore in front of your bus stop. You imagine in that moment that the store would be extremely popular.

This is your intuition at work. There are many people who have succeeded in business just by their intuition. But there are many, many more who have failed in business due to an overreliance on it.

Intuition is critical to success. But it is only a first step. Your flash of imagination as you stood at your bus stop and imagined your bookstore is like the first draft of your business plan—a rough sketch. There are as yet no details. And of course, in business, the details matter. The details may present you with obstacles you never expected. If you draw up a business plan with just your inspiration and no details, you will fail.

Instead, you need to develop metrics to measure your intuition.

Take the intuition you have and investigate it in terms of hard numbers. How many people pass by your bus stop? What are the sales of nearby stores? How many people visit bookstores at the next bus stop? What are their profits? What are the rents in your neighborhood? What are bookstore personnel costs like? Gather all this and other figures and begin to calculate the profits your bookstore might generate.

When you have filled in the details of your plan with hard numbers, take a look again at the gem of your inspiration. Look at the idea and the numbers you have developed to measure its worth.

By going through this exercise you will not only vet your first idea, but you will also begin to develop a new kind of intuition. You will start to see your idea in concert with the numbers around it. Perhaps when your idea is measured in real terms, the profit potential will not be as large as you first imagined. That does not mean you should give up. Take your detailed plan, continue to examine it, and compare it to your initial expectations. Maybe you miscalculated something. Maybe there is a way to bring those profit numbers up. As you go through this process, you will begin to have new ideas. This is your second wave of inspiration.

Now take your new model and begin the measurement process again. The numbers you need will be different each time. You will repeat this process over and over, dreaming and measuring. This is the way you will make the best use of your intuition.

Intuition is a great asset to business. But it comes to its highest purpose only when coupled with metrics. Measurement takes dreams and moves them toward reality.

## USE FRAMEWORKS

Finally, I'll address a key way we incorporate speed at Rakuten: through the use of frameworks. This is not as concrete a process as the others I've discussed. It's more of a state of mind. But when it's deployed properly, it's a huge time saver in the creation and launch of new products and services.

Successful people tend to follow winning patterns. Successful companies do the same. If you are successful in one area, think about which factors contributed and how you can execute that same strategy in another area—to replicate your success on another stage.

For example, in Rakuten Ichiba, we introduced special offers to get merchants to open shops; we introduced a points program; we instituted cost-cutting measures. Each of these contributed to the overall success of the program. We see those efforts, in retrospect, as a useful framework. We then take that framework and look for other ways to apply it. We consider it for each new business we enter—securities, travel, sports. We apply it to the new markets we enter in Europe, Asia, and North America.

This sounds simple, but many companies—especially start-ups—fail to recognize and redeploy their frameworks. They tend to ascribe their original success to some unique force of originality or creativity. And in some cases that may even be so. But the key to a quick expansion is embracing the frameworks your success has created for you.

## HOW TO ACHIEVE MUNICIPAL SPEED

Speed is good for individuals. Speed is also good for companies. It stands to reason that speed should also be good for public institutions—government offices, public utilities. Yet the concept is almost alien to many public institutions.

I believe business leaders can help in this regard. Often business leaders are asked to participate in public projects—sometimes as a funder, sometimes to offer leadership or other support. When we interact with public institutions, we should express the same need for speed that we deploy in our companies. By accepting that public institutions move slowly, we allow them to continue to do so, unchecked. We have come almost to accept this. When government officials admitted they had been slow to respond to the crisis following the March 2011 tsunami, few were surprised. It was just another example of how public institutions fail to position themselves for speed. But simply because an organization has always moved slowly does not mean it must do so forever.

## CONCLUSION

Time is more important than skill. This is a truth everyone could benefit from if they would only embrace it. It is simply a question of math. A day is twenty-four hours long. A year is 365 days. These are conditions that no one can change. What differentiates one person from another is how efficiently that person uses time. Someone who moves swiftly will always have the edge over someone who does not. The effect is as if the first individual has been granted exponentially more time to achieve his or her goals.

No matter how skilled you are, you will never beat someone who fits forty hours of work into a day when you are putting in only twenty-four hours yourself.

You do the math.

## TRY THE RAKUTEN WAY

- Make speed a corporate priority. Look for ways to reduce hours with the same zeal you would use to reduce cost. Reward speed as a corporate behavior and motivate teams to embrace it as a natural state of operations, not a tactic used only on special occasions.
- Make speed a personal priority. What are you doing now that could be done faster? Don't wait for orders; embrace speed as a personal goal.
- Allow for adjustments in progress. When you embrace speed, you must also realize that improvements will need to be made to projects in progress. Rather than wait until a project is perfected, allow for it to be launched with speed and improved along the way.

# NINE

# REWRITING THE RULES OF GIVING

## THE NEW WAVE OF COMMUNITY INVOLVEMENT

In 2003 I received a call from the mayor of my hometown of Kobe. He called to talk to me about the local soccer team.

Kobe, like many other cities in Japan, has a local soccer club. While it's great to root for international-caliber players, there is something special about being able to turn out for your home team. It's an event that brings a community together and fosters local pride.

But Kobe's local soccer team was in trouble. This was a challenging economic time in Japan, and many companies were struggling to make a profit. Kobe's primary local sponsor, a supermarket, was in financial collapse. It would not be able to continue as the soccer team sponsor. The city of Kobe itself had stepped in to run the team, but it too was unable to continue for financial reasons. The existence of the team was threatened.

The mayor of Kobe asked me to intervene and pick up this sponsorship. Although I no longer live in Kobe, my parents and sister still do and I have a strong personal attachment to the city. But that's not the only reason I said yes. I agreed to buy the team and become its financial backer for another reason, one that is bigger than my own affection for my hometown and my family ties there. I stepped in because I believe that sports teams and other cultural institutions, such as arts and music, play a special and vital role in the human experience. Business, I believe, must make more of a direct effort to be involved and supportive of these institutions. It is part of our responsibility to our communities and to our fellow human beings. It is part of the mission we all must share to improve people's lives everywhere in the world.

This may sound like a big mission for a local sports team. How can a soccer club from Kobe improve the human condition? It is more than most people expect from their cultural institutions. But it is part of my vision as a leader. In this chapter, I'll share with you why I believe business must participate in the cultural space—in sports, the arts, and all aspects of the larger community. Many companies tout their community involvement, but I believe business can do much more than it does today. It's not unusual to see a company donate money to a local charity or support a local sports team. These are considered common practices and they are acknowledged as good marketing for any firm. But I would argue that community involvement needs to transcend marketing opportunities; we must recognize the corporate role in the betterment of the human experience. I am in business not just for the success of my business, but to make the world a better place. This extends beyond the walls of my office and into many aspects of my community—from my hometown to the global landscape.

It is not just a way of "giving back." It is and must be part of our raison d'être as companies. I'll discuss how I put this belief into practice every day at Rakuten.

## GIVING BACK THROUGH CULTURAL INSTITUTIONS

If you look at the annual reports of many large companies, you will see the section in which the firm talks about how it "gives back" to the community. This support often takes the form of charitable contributions. The company may sponsor a team or an arts project. The company may facilitate its employees' volunteering and supporting good causes. Or they may simply write a check to a worthy charity. These are all good practices, and should continue. However, I believe it is wrong for corporate involvement in cultural institutions to begin and end with financial support. There is much more we can do as business leaders. There is much more we should do to contribute to the greater human community.

We can provide leadership and support for change. One of the ways we can do this is through our support of cultural institutions—not just in the form of financial support, but in our active management and participation in the activities. When we engage with cultural institutions, we engage with our communities in new and robust ways. We are not just in a business relationship with our customers, but in a deeper and more personal form of communication—one that speaks not just to commerce and economics but also to the emotions and values that run as a current through our daily lives. It is my position that a business's impact should not stop at the borders of commerce. To have a truly positive impact, a business must be willing to step out of its economic comfort zone and into the larger world in which people live, interact, and create community.

In many ways, my activities in the community reflect not just my business goals but also my larger personal goals of improving the human condition. My involvement in community service is not a "side" activity. It is fully connected to my overall goals as a businessman and as a human being.

I have said many times, throughout this book and elsewhere, that I am frustrated with the pace of change in many aspects of Japanese society. I was frustrated by our media industry's old-fashioned views when I attempted to acquire Tokyo Broadcasting System. I was so fed up with the entrenched mentality of the Japanese utility industry that I resigned—quite publicly, via Twitter—from a high-profile business trade group. In my business, I put a great deal of effort into shaking up old rules and old ways of thinking. My work in sports is yet another platform for this push.

In 2005, I was given permission to start a new Pacific League baseball franchise in Sendai. It was not easy to secure; I had to engage in a protracted public contest with another Japanese business for the right to open this franchise. It was expensive and time-consuming. What's more, baseball in Japan was in a turbulent period. We had just witnessed the very first players' strike in Japanese baseball history, and the traditional league structure was under fire.

So why did I decide to enter this arena? I felt that baseball offered yet another way to advance my philosophy that old-fashioned ways of doing business must change.

Baseball has always been very popular in Japan, but its image suffers sometimes because of its secretive business dealings. There are often rumors of misbehavior involving bribes or inflated attendance figures. This lack of transparency is a shadow on the game. It undermines the institution's ability to exert positive change in the community.

I modeled a new kind of management for my Tohoku Rakuten Golden Eagles. I brought in a new team of coaches and staff—picked specifically for their talent and their lack of ties to the "old guard" of Japanese business. I resolved to run the team with full transparency, combating the tainted history that plagued the sport. I did not tell other teams how they should operate, but I made it clear that I was planning to be different. I wanted to be open and, by doing so, to signal a new era in the game.

I encouraged team management to enter into new methods of contract and training, including everything from how the team was housed to what they ate. We did many things that angered some of the traditional power brokers in baseball. But so much of baseball had become a system of traditions and accepted practices that the game itself had suffered.

I also took my view that business should operate not just for profit but for joy and applied it in the baseball diamond. Baseball is not just a sport; it is a form of entertainment. It is a system to bring the audience joy, and this aspect of the game must not be neglected. Great players have always understood this. Consider the great Japanese home-run hitter Shigeo Nagashima. He is famous not just for his home runs but also for the gallant way he swung for the fences. It was common to see his helmet fly off when he struck out. To me, this is a sign not just of an athlete at work but also of an entertainer in his element. Even striking out, he gave the fans the emotional jolt they needed and a reason to cheer his tremendous effort at the plate. It is a true example of the way sports can and must transcend the rules of the game and involve itself in the experience of the audience. It is for their joy that the game is played.

Many of our efforts revolve around ways to turn baseball spectators into participants in the game. In the founding documents of the team you'll find our team's business philosophy: "The Baseball Entertainment Company—We are a ball club that creates thrills and inspires dreams through the game of baseball." Guided by this philosophy, the organization is striving to create a new brand of spectator culture in which fans watching the games also experience the excitement that comes from directly participating.

Events are held before the games that give local fans the chance to participate, under the banner "Spectators Becoming Participants." Events include schools and choirs singing the national anthem and traditional processions that expose people to the region's traditional art forms. Many people have taken part in these events since the team was first established. In fact, the number of participants over the years now tops fifty thousand.

The Rakuten Golden Eagles have a volunteer program that enables local fans to directly participate in ball club operations. It is the first such initiative in professional baseball and has been in place since the team's establishment. The main objective of the program is to connect with the community. Thousands of fans ages sixteen to seventy-seven have participated. Volunteers man the five Eco Stations, sorting waste and spreading the word on eco-awareness. The ball club has three categories of volunteers. In addition to "eco volunteers" who promote eco activities, the club also enjoys the services of stadium guides, who help people navigate Kleenex Stadium Miyagi during games, and medical volunteers, who provide first aid during medical emergencies.

My work in baseball was never just about baseball. These are examples not just of how I thought baseball should operate but also how all institutions in Japan should operate—with transparency and openness and contractual arrangements that support individual and team excellence. I was very aware, as

I entered the world of baseball, that the move would draw attention to me and Rakuten. I took the opportunity to demonstrate my process for entrepreneurial management and my hope for a new business model in Japan that challenges the old, entrenched ways and finds new, improved ways to move forward.

Baseball is just one of the most visible ways I interact with the community. I faced a similar process when I became president of the Tokyo Philharmonic Orchestra. This was not a position I sought out. When I was approached by the previous president, Norio Ohga, the former president of Sony, I told him that I was not sure I was well suited to the task. After all, I told Ohga, the only music I participate in is karaoke. How can I be of service to a great musical institution such as the Philharmonic?

Ohga responded this way:

"First of all," he told me, "karaoke is music. Secondly, I am certain you will figure out a way to be successful."

I am approaching this challenge in the same way I approached baseball: What can I do in service to this cultural institution that will provide leadership and a positive example to the wider community? One of the areas I am looking at now is the way in which the Philharmonic hires and retains musicians. The system is a very old and traditional contract arrangement. Is this the best way to proceed? Does this attract the best and the brightest musicians to our institution? Would a change in contract and recruiting procedures bring a positive evolution to the music we all enjoy? Whatever changes I champion, they will mirror my efforts in the sports arena: I will look for ways to change the game and improve the performance. This is the leadership role business can play in the cultural space.

## WE CAN PROVIDE INSPIRATION

It's easy to dismiss institutions such as sports and music as diversions to real life. Some say that they provide entertainment but do not play a critical role in society. I reject this notion, and consider cultural institutions to be vital. One societal function they often serve is providing inspiration. Never was this more obvious than in the months following the 2011 earthquake and tsunami.

The Rakuten Eagles are based in Sendai, where the damage from the earthquake and tsunami was most significant. The team stadium was heavily damaged: walls and walkways were cracked, and there was flooding throughout the site. Many of the team's fans were injured or displaced by the disaster. And in the early days after the event itself, fears about the fate of the nearby nuclear facility loomed large. It was a time of great physical and emotional turmoil for the region and for the country.

Amid this challenge, it was noted with great fanfare when baseball resumed in Japan—and the Rakuten Eagles took the field. It was almost exactly one month after the earthquake and tsunami. The Eagles could not play in their own damaged stadium, and had to travel to the city of Chiba to face the Chiba Lotte Marines. Many fans of the Eagles also made the trip. The Eagles players wore patches on their uniforms that encouraged fans to "stick with it," to persevere amid the challenges.

It was an inspirational game. Catcher Motohiro Shima hit a three-run homer into the left-field stands where the Eagles fans were sitting. The Eagles won 6–4, and after the final out some of the Eagles players ran out to left field to wave to their supporters.

Newspaper coverage of the game records the emotions felt by the fans that day. They believed the team gave them energy. They took strength from the win. They cheered and were cheered. It was a moment in which a sports team did far more than entertain—it inspired.

Inspiration is a role many businesses forget when they become involved with a cultural institution. They may see it as a small thing—a part of their community service to-do list that does not really affect the company's bottom line. But to the fans, a team or an orchestra or an event may mean much more. One day it's an ordinary source of entertainment, but in the weeks after a traumatic experience such as the 2011 earthquake, it can take on a far more important emotional role in people's lives.

## WE CAN DEMONSTRATE BEST PRACTICES

Much of what we do in the business community could be of use to others, but they may not have the time or inclination to come to our offices and see it. When we participate in cultural institutions in a leadership role, we create a visible platform for the knowledge we have acquired. An excellent example of this comes in the area of sustainability.

Rakuten is deeply involved in supporting and creating eco-friendly efforts. But not everyone will take the time to review our packaging standards or visit our headquarters. Our efforts in the cultural space, therefore, help us spread what we have learned. In our baseball efforts, the Rakuten Golden Eagles developed new takeout containers provided by food and beverage vendors at Kleenex Stadium Miyagi in order to reduce waste from plates, cups, chopsticks, and forks. The containers are standardized in order to make waste easier to sort and collect.

Reusable cups are also sold by Kleenex Stadium Miyagi vendors, which is another routine way fans coming to the ballpark can help protect the environment by reducing paper garbage. They can see what we have learned at Rakuten that we can now demonstrate on the wider cultural community stage.

We can go beyond basic recycling efforts and move aggressively and visibly into issues surrounding green energy. The Rakuten & Vissel Kobe Eco Project is being promoted in Kobe with the expectation that news of the project will help expand the scope of eco activity in the region. In addition to recycling efforts, this project introduced an experiment in green energy: the first floor power-generation system in spectator sports, developed by JR East Consultants Company, is being installed to convert fan cheering into electrical energy.

This system represents a new attempt to use the unique characteristics of Vissel Kobe as a spectator sport and generate power from vibrations created by the distinctive jumping that occurs when people cheer for a soccer team. The amount of electric power generated will be constantly displayed on a panel labeled with the name of the project in the concourse, which is also for the enjoyment of the supporters. The goal is to utilize the electricity as a source for some of the power consumed during the game.

## WE CAN PROVIDE PLATFORMS FOR COMMUNITY DEBATE

As a society, we must decide which direction we want to go in. We live in an age when a lot is changing very quickly, thanks to technology. How much of this change is good, and which aspects are dangerous? Many of these discussions play out in business circles. But they also surround the role and support of cultural institutions.

I have experienced this recently in my role as a baseball team owner. A team in the league was about to change ownership, and the company that wanted to step in is one that sells mobile games. I have concerns about the way mobile games charge their customers, and I worry that it's not healthy to promote this type of game to children. The game itself may be fine, but the system by which some mobile gaming companies hook customers in Japan and allow them to run up bills makes me uncomfortable.

Adults can make this decision for themselves, but children may not understand the risks. When a company owns a baseball team, it has a huge microphone with which to reach the sport's many young fans. I felt it was my obligation, as a fellow owner and businessperson, to express my concerns: Is this the message that we, as a society, want to send to our young people via a sacred form of entertainment? Others in the baseball industry may disagree, but I can use my platform as an owner to open the discussion. This is a more substantial way than sponsorship alone for the business community to participate in our larger society.

## GIVING BACK THROUGH PARTNERSHIPS

Often when I want to effect significant change in an industry or global marketplace, I make an acquisition. When you are the owner, you can execute your vision for change and improvement with speed and accuracy. It is a system that has worked well for Rakuten on the business side. But when it comes to community involvement, acquisition is not always the most suitable path. It is not always possible to be the owner of an institution that needs support and change. For that reason, my process of community involvement can't be one in which I only control the entities. There must also be a role for partnerships.

The experience of private/public partnerships can be tricky. When a business joins efforts with a nonprofit, the two must manage their differing processes and expectations in order to achieve success. Often, this requires compromise from all parties. I can't run a partnership with a nonprofit as I would a division of my company. But I can bring my own vision for success as it has emerged in the business world and apply it to the nonprofit world. Indeed, this is often the value a business leader can bring to a nonprofit institution—a vision and a pathway to a higher level of success.

One of Rakuten's most robust partnership efforts is Rakuten IT School—a Japan-wide effort to connect the next generation to the power and possibilities of the Internet. It is a part of the "Do Something Good by Rakuten" social contribution project launched on the occasion of the Rakuten Group's tenth anniversary. The programs are run by Rakuten corporate volunteers and also by Rakuten Ichiba shop owners.

The Rakuten IT School activities are designed to help children acquire a completely new sense of the potential of the Internet that they use every day. While they may be familiar with the Internet as a platform for games, virtual conversation, and even school research, Rakuten's goal is to teach them the bigger possibilities that await them in the virtual world.

The Rakuten IT School promotes collaboration between industry and academia by conducting programs that give students work experience and deepen their understanding of cooperating stores. The students get practical experience updating web pages, sending products, performing other Internet shop operations, observing the manufacturing process for mainstay products, and seeing a merchant workplace in a way not possible at their desk or on a computer screen.

Students actually get involved in devising sales strategies, constructing website shopping areas, and producing products and other operations conducted by Rakuten Ichiba shops.

The volunteer shop owners and Rakuten staff guide the activities while conveying e-commerce know-how.

To put the entire process into practice all the way through to actual sales on the site, approximately one year is spent at a single school devising sales strategies after extensive studies about consumer trends and the characteristics of the cooperating shop. Four schools are currently participating in the program. In December 2009, the Department of Information and Media at Doshisha Women's College of Liberal Arts partnered with the shop Kyoto Morisyou to launch sales of an original spice mix.

Through this collaboration, the students got the opportunity to hear feedback from real customers and learn about operating an actual Internet shop. The project is also being carried out at Ogawara Commercial High School in Miyagi Prefecture, Ino Business High School in Kochi Prefecture, and Nobeoka Commercial High School in Miyazaki Prefecture.

In addition to the e-commerce project, Rakuten holds Internet literacy courses to convey the power and potential inherent in the Internet, and ensure proper and safe Internet use. The courses are held not only for elementary school and junior high school students but also for teachers, parents, and guardians who are in a position to explain to children how to properly use the Internet.

The courses for teachers, parents, and guardians aim to impart an understanding of the psychology of children using the Internet. Discussions are held while looking at actual profile sites in an effort to promote understanding and build awareness from the children's standpoint.

Another partnership we are involved with is called Project Machi-Raku. It is a cooperative effort to engage municipal authorities in using the Internet to improve local economic conditions.

Starting with the opening of Machi-Raku Hokkaido in April 2008, we launched the regional revitalization program "Machi-Raku," which casts the spotlight on "machi" (communities) in all prefectures throughout Japan and transmits information on their respective attractions via the Internet. The Machi-Raku website is designed to entertain both local residents and visitors (or would-be visitors) and also provides information on regional specialties offered on Rakuten Ichiba as well as on tourist sites and hotels posted on the Rakuten Travel website.

The Machi-Raku website also hosts places created jointly with prefectural governors and governments, as well as municipal governments of cities, towns, and villages, to send out fresh local information. It provides access to seasonal information posted by local governments and to blogs by municipal government employees.

As part of the project, we sponsor Machi-Raku Workshops twice a year. Inviting representatives of all prefectures, we present reports on our current projects at these workshops, which also serve as occasions to share successful experiences of IT utilization conducted jointly with local governments and to create opportunities for new initiatives.

Under partnership agreements with local governments, we are also working to reinforce joint online projects and further promote IT utilization at local governments.

Why do these partnerships help us? They do not necessarily provide revenue to Rakuten—although certainly education about the Internet may well inspire more people to use our Internet services. What these partnerships do is support our fundamental core value: empowerment. If we believe in this notion of empowerment, we must believe in it both inside our company walls and outside in the community.

## GIVING BACK THROUGH CHARITY

I've focused so far on the new and creative ways in which Rakuten is involved in the community. But that does not mean that traditional methods of community support should be left behind. There is still a large and necessary role that business must play in the world of charitable donations.

When a community is in crisis, people look for ways to do some good. They look for leadership and an opportunity to participate in a positive and supportive way. Business can and must provide both this leadership and this opportunity, using its systems and infrastructure to allow individuals to combine their efforts and resources in support of others in the community.

Perhaps our most visible efforts recently centered on the aftermath of the 2011 earthquake and tsunami. I visited an evacuation shelter in Ishinomaki City, Miyagi Prefecture.

This city suffered greatly from the disaster, so I wanted to ask the people there what I could do to help. On my way to Ishinomaki City, I stopped briefly at Hiyoriyama Park. The view of the city from that vantage point revealed an area completely devastated by the tsunami. There are no words to describe it.

My conversations with those at Ishinomaki City Hall and evacuees at the junior high school now serving as an evacuation shelter helped me realize many things. First, reconstruction will be a very long road. Second, it became clearer to me that even those of us in the business community must make every effort to assist with this reconstruction. While the Great Hanshin-Awaji Earthquake remains fresh in my mind, the city of Kobe has been thoroughly reconstructed and the ruins left after the disaster in 1995 are now hard to imagine. Although the extent of the damage in the two areas differs, the success of Kobe's reconstruction makes me confident that the Tohoku region will recover from this disaster.

I have been deeply considering what Rakuten can do for Tohoku and have come to the realization that reconstruction does not simply mean restoring damaged areas to their original state. Rather, reconstruction is about building new communities. It is up to us and our children, who will inherit the future of this country, to ensure a successful reconstruction. It is vital that we give greater thought to the global environment we live in and make use of our ideas in this field for the reconstruction of Japan.

This meant doing more than raising money for Tohoku. It meant a deeper and more sustained involvement in the community.

We created a special web presence to highlight our merchants in the region and to report on their progress. We included an events calendar to spotlight news and reopenings. We offered platforms for local merchants to communicate with the world about their experiences, their businesses, and their road to recovery.

We also looked for ways to move beyond the virtual and into the hands-on daily activities of the region. We sponsored events that brought entertainment to temporary-housing residents and cooking events that brought local residents together for community meals. And like many big businesses before us, we raised money. Through our business systems we provided a way for individuals to donate money to the affected region and show their direct support for the recovery. This was hardly our first fund-raising effort. Rakuten Bank has been the nexus point for social contribution efforts throughout the world. We raised relief funds to support the families of victims and first responders of the U.S. 9/11 attacks. We raised money to support victims of earthquakes in Pakistan, Russia, Peru, and China. We raised money to support the building of an elementary school in Cambodia. This is perhaps the most traditional way business participates in community support—through the act of sponsored fund-raising. But even though it is "old-school" it must not be forgotten even as we embrace new ways to engage with the community around us. As successful businesses, our communities still look to us for monetary support.

## BUSINESS IS MORE THAN MONEY

Still, money isn't everything. I had an experience once that illuminates this issue of the role of business in the wider society. In Japan, I am well-known and often recognized in public. One night, I was at a performance with my family and someone approached me and asked to take a picture with me.

Because I was with my family at the time, I declined.

Later, my wife said to me that I'd made a mistake. "What does it cost you to stop and take a picture?" she asked. "It is a small thing, but it may have meant a lot to the person asking, and you should have said yes. It is part of the role you play in the world outside your office."

Looking back, I realize that she is right. It's not because my ego is bolstered when I am recognized or someone wants a photo with me. But my role in society does not begin and end with my business. It extends to the world around me. That's not just true for me; it's true for all of us. But I speak most specifically to those in the business world. What we do in our lives revolves around profits and losses and business issues. We need to realize that even when we leave the office, our roles as leaders remain intact. It is our job to continue to provide guidance, leadership, and inspiration in other places.

Business owners, when you come to the place in your annual report where you state how much you have "given back" to your community, ask yourself if you have given more than money. Ask yourself if you have given of your talents as a leader and as a visionary. Your business is not the only place where those talents are needed. The cultural institutions and the people who use them need those talents too.

Do more than give back. Step up.

## TRY THE RAKUTEN WAY

- Give globally. To be a global company, one must do more than do business in a location, one must be involved in all aspects of that community. This extends to community involvement and charitable giving.
- Empower through giving. Charity need not be a static act. While some events, such as earthquakes or other natural disasters, call for direct monetary giving, others need more than money—they need time and effort and expertise.
- Break the rules of community involvement. There may be rules and traditions associated with community involvement. Examine them. Some may still be applicable. Others, like other rules we have discussed in this text, may be ripe for change. Look for ways to rewrite the rules of community involvement.

# WHAT HAPPENS NEXT

## THE BRAND AS NATION

Throughout these pages, we have focused on the work of running a global business in the modern world. Before we leave this discussion, I want to speak once more about the broader mission I have undertaken. Of course, it is my intention to be successful in my business—my colleagues, my customers, and my shareholders expect this of me and they are right to do so. It is my job.

But as I move through my life as a business executive, I consider more than just the success of my own business, my own industry, even my own country. Part of my mission is to make my business and my work a positive force in the world. It is my goal not just to be successful in business but to be successful as a human being. To do this, one must always be thinking of ways to improve the world.

I remember the first time I saw clearly the road I would travel to accomplish this. It was the day I observed my colleague—then the only other member of my fledgling company—reading the *Wall Street Journal* online. I have discussed this experience previously in these pages. It was my "aha!" moment, in that I suddenly perceived with clarity the impact the Internet would have on business. But I also had a glimpse that day of the impact the Internet would have on the world—not just the business world but the entire world.

When my colleague read the *Wall Street Journal* online, the world was in the throes of change. It was certainly a moment of change for the *Wall Street Journal*. Now it could reach more customers quickly and efficiently. But it was also a moment of change for my colleague. Before the Internet, a reader in Japan might wait one or two days for the *Wall Street Journal* to arrive in Tokyo. With the Internet, access was instantaneous. My colleague was better informed and better connected to the latest business news. It could only be a positive influence on his work and his outlook for the future. He, too, had been changed.

This wave of change is one that continues to wash across the world today. Every day, time is saved, efficiencies are achieved, and connections are made thanks to the Internet. E-commerce companies were the first to understand and embrace the power of the Internet. As such, we are uniquely positioned to lead the world into the Internet future.

My goal in life is not just to make a great business, but also to make a great future. To see that evolution, we will need to see many changes.

## IN THE FUTURE, THE NATURE OF MONEY WILL CHANGE

As is the case with much of what we do, the ultimate goal is to foster positive change in the world and create a better future for humanity. We do this by recognizing an emerging reality: eventually financial services will migrate—entirely—to the Internet.

Someday soon, money as you know it now will be as quaint and collectible as a vinyl record. The Internet will centralize it all.

Money is essentially information. It is something invented by human beings that is nothing more than a promise between parties to exchange value. Money represents what we consider the value of a product or service—that is, information. And because it is mere information, it can, like all other elements of information, be hosted on the Internet.

It is only a matter of time before this happens. Virtual financial transactions are far more convenient than the paper system we have now. Already, many financial activities take place in the digital space, and it is my opinion that someday soon, all of them will go virtual. We will live in a world that no longer uses currency or paper money at all.

This is not a comfortable concept for many people. Certainly, it would be a big change from what we have today and what we have all experienced for most of our lives. And I understand that today a ten-thousand-yen bill still feels like ten thousand yen. I understand the feeling. But I also know that it is just a feeling—a sentimental holdover. We feel this way about money because it has been our experience, not because it is the only correct way to approach the concept.

Human beings have reorganized and evolved their relationship with financial services many times over the course of history. When we first began the practice of putting our money into banks, there must have been many who worried about it, who considered it dangerous or unwise. There were certainly many who were sentimental about the "old" way money was handled then and didn't want to give up their long-held patterns for this new innovation. Many generations later, we don't think twice about using a bank. It is normal to us. The same holds true about credit cards. They were considered radical in their early days and not as safe or secure as cash. Today, we use credit cards all the time. They are normal to us. Someday hosting money on the Internet will be viewed the same way.

Banks, securities, insurance—already most financial services can be accessed through the Internet. As e-commerce has grown, we have become even more used to moving money online, to pay for goods and services, to invest, and to borrow and lend. We comfortably carry plastic to pay for everything from cars to coffee.

Since the expense of delivering those services is reduced when a customer uses the Internet, it is natural that even more will follow the early adopters. The allure of a cheaper, more efficient way of doing business will not be ignored. In the not-so-distant future, every aspect of financial life will have an

Internet option. And as those options are embraced by consumers and businesses and governments, the old ways—the paper ways—will fade into history.

This evolution cannot be stopped. Just as media were unable to stop the migration of readers from paper to the Internet, so the financial services industry will also have to follow the eyeballs of consumers to the digital platform. As financial services move online, banks and securities firms will close down their brick-and-mortar branches. Business models will be reconfigured to reflect the digital reality.

## IN THE FUTURE, COMMERCE WILL NOT BE CONTAINED BY NATIONAL BORDERS

International expansion is already happening as Rakuten and other firms reach out beyond their countries of origin to do business in the global marketplace. This will remake the lives of merchants and consumers everywhere. Producers of goods and services will have the opportunity to seek customers all over the world. Many already do and many more will follow. The business of "setting up shop" will rely less and less on the location and more and more on the customer a merchant wants to reach. No longer will commerce identify with its country of origin. Instead, the world will be the marketplace.

At the same time, consumers will have access to the world's goods in new and exciting ways. Those of us living in developed economies may not fully understand the impact of this evolution, but it will mean that wherever you live, you can have access to whatever is for sale. The change will not just make money for merchants, it will improve the lives of consumers in less privileged economies. Their access to all manner of goods—from machinery to entertainment—could never have been imagined in the pre-Internet age. This will change the experience of human beings all over the world.

## IN THE FUTURE, MINDS WILL NOT BE CONSTRAINED BY NATIONAL BORDERS

Minds will follow money into the global marketplace. As customers and merchants reach out to one another across these traditional national borders, they will interact, discuss, and learn about one another in new and important ways. This process becomes not just a business transaction but also the first step in a more robust relationship. While a transaction may mark the first handshake between two individuals, the business process can then give way to a more in-depth relationship in which individuals who once considered themselves separate from one another can begin to see the connections they share.

This is one of my biggest goals as a business leader—to ensure that the expansion of minds accompanies the expansion of the marketplace. When I speak in Japan to Japanese business people, I often talk about developing this global mind-set—one that looks beyond the borders of our island and sees our future as part of an integrated whole. Commerce is the first step, but we must build upon it with richer human relationships. This is how the marketplace does more than make money—it changes the world.

The fundamental shifts of marketplace and mind currently underway suggest that in the future, the traditional role of "nation" will be greatly altered. We may still recognize these traditional borders and the cultures that go along with them. But the Internet age allows human beings to organize in new ways. People can express their allegiances in new forms and with clarity and speed. In the future, I believe, brands will be forces for human organization and inspiration—much the way nations have been throughout our history. This is not just an opportunity for brands—it is a huge responsibility. As the Internet erodes the barriers and delineations that humans have used for centuries, brands will step in with an even greater leadership role. E-commerce brands, as the first to understand the Internet, will be the first to shoulder that new challenge.

The Internet is technology with the ability not just to change commerce but also to change the human condition. For those of us at the forefront of this change, this is our challenge and our mission.

# ACKNOWLEDGMENTS

Many people contributed to the creation of this book and I would like to take this opportunity to acknowledge them and thank them for their efforts.

Quite a few Rakuten members contributed their time, skill, and hard work to this manuscript. Thank you to the CEO Office, Global Marketing and PR team, and to all the executives who contributed their time and effort in interviews and other critical tasks.

I would also like to thank those who came from outside Rakuten to join in the effort of bringing this book to into being. Thank you to my agent Leah Spiro of Riverside Creative Management for her guidance. Thank you to Emily Carleton and her team at Palgrave Macmillan for believing in the project and guiding it through the publishing experience. Thanks also to Ellen Neuborne for her help in the writing process.

Thank you to my family for their inspiration and support.

Finally, I would like to thank the many users and partners of Rakuten who believed the Internet could change the world and joined in our efforts to make that happen. I am proud to be part of your success and I look forward to the even more exciting things we will create in the future.

# INDEX

43, 52–4, 62, 66, 69–70, 75,
  86, 99, 139–41, 225

value, 43, 61, 77–8, 92–3, 120, 147,
  153–4, 219–20, 231
Vanilla Beans, 46
velocity, 179–80
"vending machine" model, 130,
  139, 144, 155, 158, 162, 165,
  167–8, 171–3, 175
vendor empowerment, 91
  *See* rice merchant story
vendor satisfaction, 118–20
Vissel Kobe, 217–18

Walmart, 161
Walkman, 107
*Wall Street Journal,* 15, 139–40, 230

waste, attacking, 180–1, 189–91,
  194–5
websites, 178–9
win-win arrangement, 46–7, 96
World Avenue, 29
World Wide Web, 28–9
  *See* Internet

Yagi, Katsuhisa, 47
Yale University, 9
Yamagishi, Yoshihiro, 143
Yammer, 123–4, 190
Yonayona brewery, 168–9
yourself, empowering, 41–4
"Y2K," 137–8
Yumetenbo, 170–1

Zappos, 91, 118